Cambridge Elements

Elements in Global Philosophy of Religion
edited by
Yujin Nagasawa
University of Oklahoma

EASTERN PHILOSOPHY AND CLASSICAL THEISM

Tyler Dalton McNabb
Saint Francis University

Erik Baldwin
Indiana University, Northwest

Shaftesbury Road, Cambridge CB2 8EA, United Kingdom

One Liberty Plaza, 20th Floor, New York, NY 10006, USA

477 Williamstown Road, Port Melbourne, VIC 3207, Australia

314–321, 3rd Floor, Plot 3, Splendor Forum, Jasola District Centre, New Delhi – 110025, India

103 Penang Road, #05–06/07, Visioncrest Commercial, Singapore 238467

Cambridge University Press is part of Cambridge University Press & Assessment, a department of the University of Cambridge.

We share the University's mission to contribute to society through the pursuit of education, learning and research at the highest international levels of excellence.

www.cambridge.org
Information on this title: www.cambridge.org/9781009660488

DOI: 10.1017/9781009660495

© Tyler Dalton McNabb and Erik Baldwin 2025

This publication is in copyright. Subject to statutory exception and to the provisions of relevant collective licensing agreements, no reproduction of any part may take place without the written permission of Cambridge University Press & Assessment.

When citing this work, please include a reference to the DOI 10.1017/9781009660495

First published 2025

A catalogue record for this publication is available from the British Library

ISBN 978-1-009-66048-8 Hardback
ISBN 978-1-009-66047-1 Paperback
ISSN 2976-5749 (online)
ISSN 2976-5730 (print)

Cambridge University Press & Assessment has no responsibility for the persistence or accuracy of URLs for external or third-party internet websites referred to in this publication and does not guarantee that any content on such websites is, or will remain, accurate or appropriate.

For EU product safety concerns, contact us at Calle de José Abascal, 56, 1°, 28003 Madrid, Spain, or email eugpsr@cambridge.org

Eastern Philosophy and Classical Theism

Elements in Global Philosophy of Religion

DOI: 10.1017/9781009660495
First published online: October 2025

Tyler Dalton McNabb
Saint Francis University

Erik Baldwin
Indiana University, Northwest

Author for correspondence: Tyler Dalton McNabb, tylerdaltonmcnabb@gmail.com

Abstract: Arguably, Classical Theism endorses the following theses: (1) God exists, (2) God is metaphysically simple, (3) God is impassible, and (4) God is wholly immutable. These theses often, though not always, lead to an endorsement of the view that God is wholly ineffable. Classical Theists, then, often see themselves as apophatic theologians. Ineffability and apophatic theology are not unknown in the great Eastern religious and philosophical traditions. In this Element, the authors explore to what extent the metaphysics of Classical Theism are consistent with the metaphysics of various Eastern traditions. After surveying each tradition, the authors argue that there is not only room for consistency, but that some of the traditions surveyed are plausibly read as endorsing Classical Theism, or at least, something not far off.

Keywords: Classical Theism, Buddhism, Daosim, Advaita Vedanta, Confucianism

© Tyler Dalton McNabb and Erik Baldwin 2025

ISBNs: 9781009660488 (HB), 9781009660471 (PB), 9781009660495 (OC)
ISSNs: 2976-5749 (online), 2976-5730 (print)

Contents

1 Classical Theism   1

2 Buddhism and Classical Theism   13

3 Hinduism and Classical Theism   25

4 Early China, Confucianism, and Classical Theism   30

5 Daoism and Classical Theism   35

   References   43

1 Classical Theism

1.1 Introduction

The goal of this Element is ambitious. In this volume, we explore to what extent the metaphysics of Classical Theism are consistent with the metaphysics of various Eastern traditions and argue that there is not only room for consistency but that some of these traditions are plausibly read as endorsing Classical Theism, or at least, something not far off. Some will feel that the journey we are about to embark on is ill-advised. "It's too ambitious. Surveying so many traditions won't do justice to any of them. There are too many moving parts. The more traditions surveyed, the more room for error." What do we have to say to these worries?

Our Element isn't the first one to survey several Eastern religions. It has been done (Harrison, 2022). Moreover, philosophers, skilled in the art of writing succinct arguments, can cover a wide range of ideas in just a few pages. Surveying the great Eastern philosophical traditions is not really any different than examining the important and diverse ideas to come out of continental philosophy of religion, another task that has been completed in another Element (Burns, 2019). As we've already mentioned, this Element surveys Eastern philosophical traditions, but it doesn't just do that. It is specifically interested in whether the central metaphysics of some of the great religious and philosophical traditions of the East can be rendered in a way that is logically consistent with the central metaphysics of Classical Theism. We argue in the affirmative.

Now, you may be thinking, 'Probably, there are no monolithic Buddhist religions or philosophical traditions, and there definitely are no such Hindu traditions. Rather, there are a multitude of particular unique traditions we lump together more or less and describe as "Buddhist" or "Hindu,"' all the while assuming that these categorizations fall under the rubric of Indian religion. So, how can one show that the central metaphysics endorsed by Buddhist or Hindu traditions are consistent with the central metaphysics of Classical Theism? In response to these concerns, note that our thesis is rather modest. We take it that the metaphysics of *some* Eastern philosophical traditions we typically and correctly refer to as Buddhist or Hindu can be rendered in a logically consistent manner with the metaphysics of a certain stripe of Classical Theism. We are not arguing that all or most or even a large percentage of particular traditions that are taken to be branches of Hinduism and Buddhism are consistent with Classical Theism. Instead, for each tradition, our approach is to identify a consensus among (a certain subset of) experts as to what constitutes those minimal metaphysical commitments that are central to each tradition. For example, if noteworthy experts in Buddhist Philosophy such as Jay Garfield, Jan Westerhoff, and David Burton all say that Buddhists must believe in the interdependence thesis (more on this thesis soon), then the interdependence thesis must be rendered logically consistent with Classical Theism, at least if our thesis is to remain viable. But now we're getting ahead of ourselves. We've already used the term 'Classical Theism' several times without defining it. To that task we now turn.

1.2 Classical Theism

In everyday conversation, it's not always easy to know how a term is being used. This can lead to considerable confusion. For instance, the word 'coke' is often used as shorthand for Coca-Cola but in some circles, it more typically refers to cocaine. So, if Tyler says, 'Do you have any Coke?' and Erik takes Tyler to be asking for the soft drink formally called Coca-Cola, Tyler and Erik would be using 'Coke' in the same way. In this conversational context, 'Coke' is being used univocally. In an altogether different context, should Erik take it that Tyler is asking for cocaine, Tyler and Erik are using the term 'Coke' equivocally. That is, they do not attach the same meaning to the utterance 'Coke' but are in fact talking about two completely different things. This misunderstanding would arise only in particular contexts, such as certain kinds of parties or get-togethers, but similar confusions about the meanings of important terms often arise in theological and philosophical contexts. Terms such as 'existence,' 'being,' 'Being,' 'nothing,' 'no-thing,' 'emptiness,' and 'Classical Theism' are used in a variety of ways, so we need to take particular care to sort out what we mean when using them. In addition to paying attention to how language use involves univocal and equivocal meanings, we also need to pay attention to how we use words to express analogies.

We use analogical language when we compare things from different classes and note that they share a similar feature. We make analogies for a host of reasons. They are used in literature and song to artfully call to our attention some matter of interest or importance. For instance, when Sheryl Crow sings 'Everyday is a winding road,' she effectively calls to our attention how the unpredictably of life is comparable to the twists and turns of an unfamiliar road. Roads have literal twists and turns, whereas our lives unfold in unexpected and unpredictable directions in ways that are analogous to those roads (Crow, 1996). Along similar lines, in Frank Herbert's classic science fiction novel *Dune*, we read that Paul Atreides, aka Maud'dib, not only has the ability of prescience but can also 'see' multiple future possibilities and is able to make choices to try to bring about a desirable possible timeline or to avoid an undesirable one. When speaking of this ability to others, Paul describes his knowledge of far-off future possibilities as like unto seeing patterns in the currents of a swirling ocean. In contrast, he describes his knowledge of near future events as analogous to knowing that opening and going through various doors would lead to different outcomes (Herbert, 1965).

In religious and philosophical discourse, we often employ analogies to explicitly predicate attributes to things that belong to different classes. Analogical predication doesn't involve the equivocal use of a term, where the relevant word has radically different referents, but it doesn't pick out the same exact referent either. For instance, when we use terms like 'health' and 'being' analogically to say different things, there is a similar concept that is being employed. For example, while we say that a cat is healthy and that the food it eats is healthy, we attribute 'health' to the cat and to its food in different senses. The cat is healthy in a primary sense by being the bearer of health and the food is healthy in a secondary sense by contributing to the health of the cat but it is nevertheless true to say of both that cat and the food that they are healthy.

Before diving any deeper into analogical predication, consider Aristotle's argument that 'being,' like 'health,' is said in many ways. In *Metaphysics* 1003^a33-1003^b10, he writes:

> Something is said to be in many ways, however, but with reference to one thing and one nature – that is, not homonymously. Rather, just as what is healthy all has reference to health, one by safeguarding it, another by producing it, one by being an indication of health, another because it is a recipient of it, and what is medical has reference to the craft of medicine (for one thing is said to be medical by possessing the craft of medicine, another by being naturally well-disposed to it, another by being a result of the craft of medicine), and we shall find other things that are said to be in similar ways to these, so, too, something is said to be in many ways, but all with reference to one starting-point. For some things are said to be because they are substances, others because they are a route to substances, or else by being passings away, lacks, or qualities of substance, or productive or generative either of substance or of things that are said to be with reference to substance, or denials of these or of substance (that is why we say even of not being that it *is* not being) (Aristotle, 2016).

Among other things, what Aristotle says here goes to show that we need an account of analogical predication to account for the various ways we attribute 'health' to things and the various ways we talk about the ways things are said to be. Inspired by Aristotle, Aquinas maintains that analogical predication permeates our talk about God. In *The Summa Theologica*, Aquinas argues against both univocal and equivocal accounts of predication. His argument against univocal predication is as follows:

> Univocal predication is impossible between God and creatures. The reason of this is that every effect which is not an adequate result of the power of the efficient cause, receives the similitude of the agent not in its full degree, but in a measure that falls short, so that what is divided and multiplied in the effects resides in the agent simply, and in the same manner; as for example the sun by exercise of its one power produces manifold and various forms in all inferior things. In the same way ... all perfections existing in creatures divided and multiplied, pre-exist in God unitedly. Thus when any term expressing perfection is applied to a creature, it signifies that perfection distinct in idea from other perfections; as, for instance, by the term "wise" applied to man, we signify some perfection distinct from a man's essence, and distinct from his power and existence, and from all similar things; whereas when we apply to it God, we do not mean to signify anything distinct from His essence, or power, or existence. Thus also this term "wise" applied to man in some degree circumscribes and comprehends the thing signified; whereas this is not the case when it is applied to God; but it leaves the thing signified as incomprehended, and as exceeding the signification of the name. Hence it is evident that this term "wise" is not applied in the same way to God and to man. The same rule applies to other terms. Hence no name is predicated univocally of God and of creatures. (Aquinas, I., q. 13, a.5)

His argument against equivocal predication goes thus:

> Neither ... are names applied to God and creatures in a purely equivocal sense ... Because if that were so, it follows that from creatures nothing could be known or demonstrated about God at all; for the reasoning would always be exposed to the fallacy of equivocation ... Therefore it must be said that these names are said of God and creatures in an analogous sense, i.e. according to proportion. (Aquinas, I., q. 13, a.5)

Having argued against both extremes, echoing Aristotle, Aquinas argues for his preferred middle view, analogical predication:

> Now names are thus used in two ways: either according as many things are proportionate to one, thus for example "healthy" predicated of medicine and urine in relation and in proportion to health of a body, of which the former is the sign and the latter the cause: or according as one thing is proportionate to another, thus "healthy" is said of medicine and animal, since medicine is the cause of health in the animal body. And in this way some things are said of God and creatures analogically, and not in a purely equivocal nor in a purely univocal sense. For we can name God only from creatures. Thus whatever is said of God and creatures, is said according to the relation of a creature to God as its principle and cause, wherein all perfections of things pre-exist excellently. Now this mode of community of idea is a mean between pure equivocation and simple univocation. For in analogies the idea is not, as it is in univocals, one and the same, yet it

is not totally diverse as in equivocals; but a term which is thus used in a multiple sense signifies various proportions to some one thing; thus "healthy" applied to urine signifies the sign of animal health, and applied to medicine signifies the cause of the same health. (Aquinas, I., q. 13, a.5)

So, when Eden says there is a 'foundation' to our beliefs and there is a 'foundation' to the house, she doesn't use 'foundation' in the same exact way. She is not completely equivocating as when Tyler asks Erik for Coke and Erik thinks Tyler wants drugs. There being a 'foundation' for her beliefs and there being a 'foundation' for her house, retain some connection as to how we should conceive the relevant object. There is obviously a difference however, between what epistemologists call a foundation and what contractors call a foundation. There isn't straight forward univocity. For the scholastics, there is also an awareness that analogy comes in degrees determined in part by the relevant type of analogy.

Now, armed with analogical predication, when Classical Theists say that God exists, is all-powerful, or all-knowing, they aren't using these terms univocally. Consider power. Humans have various kinds of powers, such as the power to lift heavy objects, the power to perform mathematical operations, and the power of imagination. All of these human powers are limited in scope. God's power is not so limited. As Aquinas puts it, God can do all things that are possible with respect to his active power, his power to cause or to act (Aquinas, Part 1, Q. 25, A. 3.). In contrast, that God is immovable or impassible are among God's passive powers. That is, God's being such that he is immovable puts limits on what sorts of causes he is susceptible to and, similarly, God's being such that He is impassible puts limits on the ways in which he can be acted upon. Being able to be caused to go out of existence, for instance, is something that God isn't susceptible to. God doesn't happen to exist, for His existence is metaphysically necessary.[1] Because nothing can cause God *not* to exist, His being unable not to

---

[1] It's worth noting that there are various accounts of the metaphysical necessity of God. Gottfried Leibniz maintains that the existence of contingent things must be accounted for by something that non-contingent, i.e., a necessary being, " ... a being in whom essence involves existence ... in whom possible being is sufficient for actual being." This necessary being is God. See Leibniz, *Die philosophischen Schriften. 7 vols, Ed.C. I. Gerhardt.* (Hildesheim: Georg Olms, 1965), VI 614/ AG 218. According to Richard Swinburne, "God exists" is necessary in the sense that God does not depend on himself or anything else to exist and no agent or natural law causes or explain his existence. God's existence is a brute fact. See Swinburne, 1977, p. 267. According to Alvin Plantinga, "God exists" is metaphysically necessary in a stronger sense. He maintains that because God is maximally great, he displays maximal greatness in every possible world. If God is maximally great in this way, then God can't possibly not exist. See Plantinga, 1992. Aquinas goes further. He maintains that God is an uncaused necessary being that cannot undergo substantial change, thus God cannot not exist (*Summa Theologia,* 1, Q1, A1; 1, Q3, A4; 1, Q9, A1). The existence of God accounts of the existence of all other beings, and God's power preserves all things in existence (1, Q104, A1). For more on Thomas Aquinas's account of the metaphysical necessity of God, see Wahlberg, 2024, pp. 131–152; Robson, 2012, pp. 219–241.

exist isn't a limitation on any power in God. Similarly, it is not inconsistent with God's omnipotence that He can't make an impossible object, such as a round square, to exist. This inability doesn't count as limitation on God's power for actualizing contradictions is not something that is logically possible to do. The difference between human power and God's power is not a matter of degree but of quality. It's not as if we humans just had more power then we would be incapable of being acted on or somehow transcend the causal powers to which we are susceptible. When we speak thus of power in God and power in humans, we employ analogical predication. That is, God and humans both have power, not in the same sense but in an analogous one. In contrast, if terms like "power" and "goodness" *are* used univocally, then, arguably, we must say that God and humans are on the same ontological level, that the differences in power between God and humanity are a matter of degree. This naturally leads to the conclusion that God, like any human person, is a composite being, a being with an essence, or nature, and various essential and accidental properties. Classical Theists deny this. They maintain that God is metaphysically simple, utterly without parts or composition. Following Thomas Aquinas, one way to arrive at this conclusion is to consider and reject the ways in which it could be said that God is composite.[2] Another and perhaps more intuitive way to motivate the view is to call attention to Aquinas's view that creatures possess properties by exemplifying them and that property exemplification involves a created being resembling God in a delineated and finite way. In contrast, we can't comprehend the being of God precisely or fully adequately. God, the source and perfect exemplar of all creaturely perfections, possesses no properties. Put another way, because created beings exemplify properties only by means of participation in the being of God, and since only created things exemplify properties in this way, God neither possesses nor exemplifies properties.[3] Suffice to say, we maintain that, strictly speaking, it is false to say that God has properties, it is nevertheless appropriate to talk as if God has the property of existing, or being all-powerful, or all-knowing, and the like, so long as we stipulate that these predications are really just shorthand descriptions that express one and the same reality of God. In God, there is no difference in his being powerful, good, or beautiful, for in God there is no distinction between his essence and his existence (Gilson, 1956, p. 107).

Sometimes, critics of Classical Theism contend that these claims lead to a purportedly fatal objection, one often encountered in conversations at philosophical gatherings and mixers if not in print. 'Classical Theism endorses

---

[2] We make no attempt to repeat that massive endeavor here but refer the reader to *Summa Theologica* Book 1 question 3 "On the Simplicity of God."

[3] For more on this line of argument, see Panchuk, 2021, pp. 385–402.

Divine Simplicity, according to which God has no properties. But if God has no properties, God lacks the property of existence. Thus, Classical Theists can't affirm the proposition 'God exists' but are rather forced to affirm it to be false. But this is absurd. Thus, Classical Theism must be false.' While this objection may seem powerful, we maintain it has little force and rests on crucial misunderstandings and ignores important distinctions. The debate hangs on disagreement about how to understand the notion of existence. Both Classical Theists and their critics agree that cars exist, that Luka Doncic exists, or that the book that you are reading exists. Such existence claims are unproblematic. In contrast, Classical Theists maintain that God does not exist in the manner that everyday things do. For example, those of the Blackfriar Thomistic Tradition deny that God is a thing.[4] Similar to how members of Platonic and Neo-Platonic traditions affirm that the form of the Good 'is not being, but superior to it in rank and power' (Plato, 1997, 509b), these and other Thomists maintain that God's being is not like that of everyday beings, for such things exist only because of God's sustaining power. Unlike beings that have their existence imparted to them, God exist *a se*, that is, through himself. God's existence isn't imparted from another, neither does it depend on or proceed from something external to God. Anselm argues that God exists not through something else, for then his existence would be dependent on that through which he exists, and clearly it is false that he exists through nothing, for it is impossible for anything to exist through nothing. Equally obviously, God doesn't cause himself to exist; it's not as if at one time God didn't exist and then somehow caused his own existence. The only possibility left is that God exists through himself. Anselm goes on to explain that the best way to understand how God exists through himself is to consider the relations between 'to shine' and 'shining' (Anselm, 1996, Chapters V and VI). Should we turn on a night light for an inquisitive child, she is likely to ask where the light comes from. We may truthfully say in response that the light from the nightlight lights up the room, that is, that the light shining in the room exists through the shine of the nightlight. Analogously, God's supreme nature is related to his existence in a way similar to the shine of the light that lights up the room.

For Classical Theists, God is not a being but rather being itself; God's existence is inseparable from his essence. To mark the difference between these two modes of existence, namely, the creaturely mode and the creator mode, we in accordance with the mode of being proper to God say that God exists*, and that, in accordance with the mode of being proper to created things

---

[4] This view is sometimes referred to as Grammatical Thomism. See, for instance, Casti and Hewitt, 2020, pp. 1–7; Hewitt.

such as people and books, that they exist. Since we use the word 'exist' every day to talk about things we encounter in the course of our lived experience, and we do not directly experience the being of God in the same way, we will say that only God exists*. Note that 'existing*' isn't 'existing' but is rather an analogue for 'existing.' While we are acquainted with and so can comprehend things that exist on the creaturely mode of existence, being creatures ourselves, we are not so acquainted with the uncreated being of God. The mode of existence that is unique to the creator is not something that we are acquainted with. It is not something we can comprehend. But we can have an adequate conceptualization of it by means of analogy. Using analogical reasoning and employing analogical predication on the basis of things we experience at our level or mode of existence, we extend our thinking towards God's mode of being. This enables us to have a limited understanding of God's mode of being that, for all its shortcomings, is sufficiently adequate. Putting the point both poetically and succinctly, we shall say that created beings are things. In contrast, God is uniquely unique; God is not a thing, since God doesn't possess properties, nor is He a property.[5] God is literally no-thing.[6] To say that God is no-thing is to say that God is beyond existence in the sense that God is the very foundation of existence and that which makes the realm of existing things possible.[7] God's existence is the ultimate answer to why there is something rather than nothing. Things exist only because God exists.

Because we are not acquainted with and so cannot comprehend the uncreated being that is God, Classical Theists maintain that God is wholly ineffable. Like the Eastern Christian Fathers of old express the point, we cannot know or fully comprehend God's essence.[8] That God is not a being but rather the ground of all

---

[5] *Contra*, Plantinga who argues that if God exists and is simple then he must be identical to a property. This of course assumes univocal predication pertains to our talk about God's being. As we've made clear, we reject that. Plantinga, 1980. For a detailed refutation of Plantinga's objection, see Lamont, 1997, pp. 528–531.

[6] David Bentley Hart seemingly endorses referring to God as a no-thing in *Experience of God: Being, Consciousness, Bliss* (New Haven: Yale University Press, 2014), 107.

[7] For more on this point, see McNabb and Baldwin, 2022, pp. 21–22.

[8] St. Gregory of Nysa, for example, states the following: "And by this deliverance the Word seems to me to lay down for us this law, that we are to be persuaded that the Divine Essence is ineffable and incomprehensible: for it is plain that the title of Father does not present to us the Essence, but only indicates the relation to the Son. It follows, then, that if it were possible for human nature to be taught the essence of God, He Who will have all men to be saved and to come to the knowledge of the truth 1 Timothy 2:4 would not have suppressed the knowledge upon this matter. But as it is, by saying nothing concerning the Divine Essence, He showed that the knowledge thereof is beyond our power, while when we have learned that of which we are capable, we stand in no need of the knowledge beyond our capacity, as we have in the profession of faith in the doctrine delivered to us what suffices for our salvation." Gregory of Nysa, *Against Eunomius*, Translated by Ogle and Wilson, 1893. Revised and edited for New Advent by Kevin Knight. www.newadvent.org/fathers/290102.htm.

being is mysterious. It's one thing to know the essence of a human, say a rational animal, but it is a whole other thing to know the essence of what is beyond the realm of existent things.

With this background in place, we now elucidate what we mean by saying God is not a thing by giving the following statement of equivalence:

> T is a thing if and only if T can possess a property or T is a property.

It isn't just that God lacks properties or is beyond existence, Classical Theists think that God is wholly impassible. That is to say, God causally effects all things, but no things have any causal effect on Him. And while things have a real relation to God, God is not really related to things. We humans, being things, therefore, cannot cause any change in God whatsoever. Moreover, Classical Theists think that God is wholly immutable; not only can nothing cause a change in God, God cannot cause a change in Himself. The Scholastics maintain that for a thing to change, the thing must have potentiality to be a different way, and there must be something already in act that moves upon the potential to change.[9] For example, a glass of Dr. Pepper is potentially hot. But it won't become hot unless something with heat moves upon its potential to be hot (e.g., fire). When something goes from potency to actuality, we have change. Classical Theists think that God is pure actuality; there is no potency in God. So, God cannot change. Another argument given for God's immutability is that change requires space and time, and since God is outside of space and time, God does not change.

Let's sum up the central theses of Classical Theism:

1) Divine Simplicity (DS): God is not made up of parts.
2) Divine Impassibility (DI): No thing can cause a change in God.
3) Divine Atemporality: (DA): God is outside of space and time.
4) Divine Immutability (DIU): God cannot change in any way.

Pulling all this together, for the purposes of this Element, when we say Classical Theism, we mean the conjunction of DS, DI, DA, and DIU. We also take it that DS entails that God is not a thing. Here's the argument. If DS is true, then God, not made up of parts, has no properties. All things have properties or are properties. Thus, if DS is true, it follows that God is not a thing.

Classical Theism can be contrasted with Neo-Classical Theism. Neo-Classical Theists primarily view God as a being among other beings, though God is still the explanation of all other beings and is the greatest conceivable being. God is a person, usually understood in a univocal sense of the term. Neo-Classical

---

[9] See, for example, Feser, 2014.

Theists typically view God as a being in time, even if, *sans* creation, He is timeless (Craig, 2001). God is understood to possess the standard Omni properties – omnipotence, omniscience, omnipresence, and the like – even if its proponents offer nontraditional analyses of them. We can thus understand Neo-Classical Theism as the denial of one or more of the central theses of Classical Theism. For instance, *contra* DS, Neo-Classical Theists affirm that God is complex, having parts that are not identical to himself, such as properties, intentions, propositional attitudes, and the like. *Contra* DI and DIU, things can have a casual effect on God and it is possible for God to be changed by things and for God to bring about changes in himself. And, *contra* DA, God is temporal, being inside space and time.[10] Neo-Classical Theism leaves it an open question whether and if so how God has knowledge of future contingents.

Against Classical Theism, Neo-Classical theists argue that certain aspects of traditional Judeo-Christian belief, including commonsense readings of the Jewish and Christian Scriptures, conflict with Classical Theism and so fail to cohere with the Christian Tradition generally (Peckham, 2021 and 2024). Others object that the view entails a troubling modal collapse, briefly, that Classical Theism entails necessitarianism, that everything exists necessarily (Mullins, 2016). For a general defense of Classical Theism against these sorts of coherence and conflict objections see Duby (2016) and for a response to the modal collapse objection see Tomaszewski (2019). See Feser (2022) for a specifically Thomistic response to Neo-Classical Theism's defenders. Alvin Plantinga objects that if God is identical to each of his properties, then each of his properties is identical to his other properties, and it follows that God has but one property. But if God has a singular property and is identical with his property, it follows that God *is* a property, an abstract object and not a person (Plantinga, 2007). Responding to Plantinga, John Lamont argues that Aquinas would deny that God could possibly be an abstract object (Lamont, 1997). If by 'property' we mean an abstract object that exists outside of space-time, Aquinas denies that there are any such things. He maintains that all actual things or objects must have a location in space-time. According to Aquinas, properties exist but only in actual things; there are no unexemplified or abstract objects existing immaterially and without causal powers. In short, we may say that Plantinga's objection falls flat because it imports a notion of 'property' that is inconsistent with Aquinas's core metaphysics. Similarly, one could argue that Plantinga's argument assumes univocal language,

---

[10] For a similar analysis of Neo-Classical Theism and Classical Theism, see Sijuwade, 2021, pp. 1–3.

which, as we noted, Aquinas rejects. At best, God wouldn't be a property but like a property. But even Neo-Classical Theists can think this.

1.3 Classical Theism and Paradox

While some of the implications of Classical Theism seem hard to grasp, others apparently have more apparent paradoxical consequences. But even these paradoxical features are not without their merits, for they reveal that Classical Theism has surprising strengths. For example, William Rowe has argued there are instances of gratuitous evil, evils such that an all-good and all-powerful God could have prevented without precluding some greater good or permitting some comparable evil. Since God would likely prevent such evils if He existed, the existence of such evils counts as evidence against the existence of God (Rowe, 1979, p. 336). But there are reasons for thinking that we are not well-suited epistemically to make well-grounded judgments about what sorts of evils are necessary for bringing about some greater good. For example, Michael Bergmann points out that while theists aren't skeptical about God's existence, they are often skeptical about whether our sample of possible goods and evils, namely, the good and evils of which we are aware, is representative of the possible goods and evils that there are. Because of the relatively meager samples of goods and evils that are epistemically available to us, and because of our ignorance of relations between the occurrence of this or that evil and how it may or may not be necessary in order to bring about some greater good, we are unable to determine whether this or that evil is inconsistent with the Goodness of God. It follows that we are unable to know what sort of reasons God could have for permitting such evils (Bergmann, 2011, pp. 377–378). On the metaphysical side of the matter, Brian Davies has argued extensively that since God is not a being among other beings, and since our language about God is at best analogical, we anthropomorphize God when we say what God would likely do action 'A' in some given instance (Davies, 2006). Sure, we can know what rational agents like us would do, and we may know what morally good rational agents like us would do, but why think we are in any position to know what God, who is beyond existence, would do? Again, God is not really good but only good*. Similarly, God is not an agent but agent*, and God doesn't cause, He causes*. Granted, we might say that God is a moral agent or that God has obligations, but at best, these claims are only analogically true. For all that, there are, we think, good reasons for thinking that God is not subject to the same moral rules and obligations that we humans are (see Murphy, 2017).

For similar reasons, James Anderson argues that paradoxes that emerge from discussing God's nature have unarticulated equivocations (Anderson, 2007, pp. 93–107). If one endorses analogical language, there will always be some part of a predicate that doesn't map on to God as it would map on to creatures. Michael DeVito and Tyler Dalton McNabb use this insight from Anderson to argue for the mysterian resolution to the problem of divine foreknowledge and human freedom (DeVito and McNabb, 2021). While it might be true that infallible foreknowledge entails that S can do no other, the same might not be true when it comes to infallible foreknowledge*. That is, when we look at the problem of foreknowledge and freedom, we typically speak of God's having knowledge and belief in an anthropomorphic way, a way in which humans would be said to have knowledge and belief. If instead we predicate infallible foreknowledge to God in only an analogical way, it isn't clear if the same ramifications follow. Appealing to mysterianism has its advantages and it seems natural if God is not a member of the realm of existence things.

One way to target the sort of mysterianism we engage is to target whether it is coherent to reject univocal predication. Dun Scotus does just this when he famously objects to the Thomistic account of divine simplicity. He argues that talk about God can't be analogical all the way down. That is, analogical talk about God requires univocal meanings to hold for at least some of our crucial terms.[11] Here is the problem put more formally:

(1) Analogical language requires there be similarity between the objects being compared.
(2) There cannot be genuine similarity between two objects without univocity.
(3) Therefore, analogical language requires univocity.

One response to this objection is to concede the premises for sake of argument but deny that God is an object that can be compared to another object. That is, since God is not an object, he transcends objectification. This response grants that premises (1) and (2) are true but maintains that its truth is inapplicable to God and His mode of existence*. It would have us read (3) to specifically speak of objects. If (3) ought to be read as to include that which is beyond being, the argument simply isn't valid. (1) and (2) can be true and yet, (3) could be false. The way to save the argument is to read (3) as just applying to objects. But doing this, the argument becomes irrelevant for Classical Theists of the stripe we have in mind. Once again, objections like this fail to hit the mark because they assume that God is an object among other objects.[12]

---

[11] As an example, see *Ordinatio* I, d.3, q.1.
[12] While we are on the topic of objections from Scotus, what are we to make of Scotus' argument that a valid argument requires univocity to preserve the argument's validity? Moreover, even if we could preserve validity without univocity, we need some sort of explanation for why some arguments that make use of analogical language are valid while other arguments that make use of

It is exceedingly difficult and even unnatural to refrain from anthropomorphizing God in our philosophical and theological discourse. But once we recognize the full extent of what it means for God to *not* be a being, many of the traditional objections to belief in God simply dissolve. Objections against Classical Theism will often smuggle in notions of univocity. OK, enough about smuggling and drugs. We are now in the position to clarify and outline this Element.

1.4 What Remains

Recall that in this Element, we argue that the central metaphysics of some Eastern philosophical traditions can be rendered such that they are consistent with the central metaphysics of a certain flavor of Classical Theism. Recall, too, that we are not arguing that this or that particular religion is wholesale consistent with Classical Theism, but we rather are looking specifically at the central metaphysics of the relevant traditions. We go about establishing our thesis by surveying the central metaphysics of Buddhism, Advaita Vedānta Hinduism, Confucianism, and Daoism. We now turn to engaging Buddhism.

2 Buddhism and Classical Theism
2.1 Introduction to Buddhist Metaphysics

Buddhism is typically interpreted, especially in the West, as an atheistic or nontheistic religious tradition (Patil, 2009). Paul Williams, a world-renowned scholar of Buddhism, left his Buddhist tradition and embraced Catholicism, in part, because he determined that Buddhism has no room for God (Williams, 2002). Asanga Tilakartne references *The Middle Length Discourses of the Buddha* to argue that the Buddha seemed to think there was no overlord of the world, that is, no creator, governor, or sustainer of things (Tilakartne, 2016, pp. 100–101). Specifically, Tilakartne appeals to *Sutta* 82 where we read, '[Life in] any world has no shelter and no protector' (Bhikku Nanamoli and Bhikkhu Bodh, 2016, p. 688). In *The Long Discourses*, or *Dīgha Nikāya*, Tilakartne argues that the concept of God is presented as untenable. Later Buddhist traditions are even more explicit in denying that there is a creator God. Tilakartne argues that the primary reason why Buddhism is inconsistent with theism is that the path to *nirvāṇa* is godless. The very nature of the path '... is

---

analogical language are not valid. Thomas Sutton argues that analogy is degreed. Sometimes an analogical use of a term doesn't preserve validity because some arguments lack the relevant proportionate unity. Analogical uses of terms which are sufficiently relevant will preserve the truth value in the conclusion. See discussion of Sutton's view in D'Ettore, 2019, pp. 33–60.

based on the assumption that there is no saviour God' (Tilakaratne 2016, p. 101).

David Burton puts it like this:

> Christians believe in a creator God whereas Buddhists do not. Most Christians regard Jesus as uniquely salvific whereas Buddhists do not share this conviction. The Buddhist soteriological aim is nirvana, which seems very different from the Christian conception of heaven. Buddhists usually believe in Karma and rebirth whereas Christians normally do not, and so on. (Burton 2017, p. 179)

So, we have the so-called absence of God (i.e., passages which don't speak of God) in both foundational Buddhists texts and the Four Noble Truths, and we have a couple of sayings from the Buddha's discourses that could be interpreted in a way that rules out theism. So far it is not looking good for those who think that theism and Buddhism are logically consistent. That this is so apparently rules out the possibility of someone accepting, at least reasonably so, both Buddhism and Classical Theism. We suppose that someone could agree with the Four Noble Truths and the Eightfold Path and yet reject certain parts of the Pāḷi canon. For instance, one may take the Buddha to be a prophet who reveals to us how to significantly decrease the amount of suffering in our world but also maintain that the Buddha was not right about everything he taught. For example, it could be argued that those parts of his metaphysics that *are* in conflict with Classical Theism are false or are not essential features of Buddhism. Or perhaps one might think that the Buddha is a saintly figure who shares important truths with the world but the parts of the Pāḷi canon that leave no room for theism are in fact out of step with the teachings of the historical Buddha. Taking this route, one maintains that there is a difference between what the historical Buddha taught and what the Pāḷi canon teaches. By rejecting the Pāḷi canon, a Buddhist who wants to be a theist can in fact be a theist. But a problem remains, one which we take to be more fundamental than these textual and historical issues, one that apparently prevents Buddhists from being theists. The problem relates to the central metaphysical theses of Buddhism being inconsistent with the existence of God, or anything relevantly similar. The eminent philosopher of Buddhism, Jay Garfield, summarizes the 'essentials' of Buddhism below:

> Suffering (*dukkha*) or discontent is ubiquitous in the world ...
> The origin of *dukkha* is in primal confusion about the
> fundamental nature of reality, and so its cure is at bottom a
> reorientation toward ontology and an awakening (*bodhi*) to the
> actual nature of existence.
> All phenomena are impermanent (*anitya*), interdependent
> (*pratītya-samutpāda*) and have no intrinsic nature (*śūnya*) ...

> Fundamental confusion is to take phenomena, including
> preeminently oneself, to be permanent, independent and to have
> an essence or intrinsic nature (*svabhāva*).
> The elimination (*nirvāṇa*), or at least the substantial reduction
> of *dukkha* through such reorientation, is possible.
> An ethically appropriate orientation toward the world is
> characterized by the cultivation of *mudita* (an attitude of rejoicing
> in the welfare and goodness of others, of *mettā*) beneficence toward
> others, and especially of *karuṇā* (commitment to act for the welfare
> of sentient beings). (Garfield, 2014, p. 2)

Notice the crucial metaphysical theses in these paragraphs, namely, that all phenomena are impermanent, interdependent, and lack own-being. What do these claims amount to?

Jan Westerhoff describes the interdependence thesis in the following way: 'An object *a* existentially depends on objects falling under the property F iff necessarily, if *a* exists there exists something falling under F' (Westerhoff, 2010, p. 26). David Burton puts it as, 'All entities have a dependently arisen and conceptually constructed existence ... " (Burton, 2017, p. 36). Roughly, the idea is that all things, objects, phenomena, and the like are causally and conceptually dependent. We shall use each of these three terms interchangeably. Consider the following example of causal dependence. A plant presently depends on its temporally prior state of being a seed. It also depends on the ground, dirt, rain, sunlight, and so on. These things, of course, in turn depend on other things to be the sort of things that they are, the earth, and so on. In like manner, all things are causally dependent on other things. Consider now the concept of a plant. In order to understand what a plant is, we must understand, at least in part, what a living organism is and what petals and stems are. Moreover, to understand what a living organism is, we need to understand the contrasting concept of 'non-living thing' as well. In like manner, none of our concepts are atomistic but rather grow and become intwined into a web or net of interconnected and interdependent concepts. It is important to note that this sort of dependence isn't merely conceptual but also metaphysical. That is, if the sun didn't exist, then neither would the flower, and the flower wouldn't exist as the sort of thing it is if it lacked its petals.

The impermanence thesis is roughly the view that all things are impermanent. Generally, it is understood to imply that things do not retain their identity from moment to moment but rather have momentary existence. Here is an argument for the view. Buddhists maintain whenever a thing undergoes change, however subtle, it undergoes substantial change. Why think this? You might recall from your modern philosophy class Leibniz's Law of Identity, which states that in order for A to equal B, A and B need to share the same exact properties.[13] Now consider the following: If Clare, Tyler's miniature goldendoodle, loses a property at time T, Clare before T and Clare at T do not share the same properties and are therefore not identical. Clare is no longer identical to Clare prior to T, but is a brand-new Clare, since Clare before T fails to preserve all of her properties (Garfield, 2014, p. 42). It may *look* like Clare continues to exist from moment to moment, but that is simply not the case. Not only does Clare[1] cease to be given a moment's passing, but, given the interdependence thesis, we know that Clare[1] wasn't even an independent substance in the first place. Generalizing the point, for any time you pick, Clare lacks own being, or *svabhāva*. So, with the possible exception of *dharmas* (i.e., the basic metaphysical building blocks of reality), according to Buddhism, all things are truly empty of own-being.[14]

Having explicated these important metaphysical theses, we are now in a position to see the obstacles that seem to preclude Buddhists from accepting Classical Theism. If God is a thing, and if the interdependence thesis applies to all things, then we can't suppose that God exists *a se*. Rather, God metaphysically depends on other things for His existence. It also seems plausible that, if God depends on His creation for His existence, that if His creation is in time, God would be as well. Thus, if God is temporally related to things, God, too, gains and loses properties. If God is a thing, then the impermanence thesis likewise applies to God. Given the impermanence thesis, it follows that God has momentary existence: for every passing moment, we have a different God. While this sort of being may be consistent with the existence of the God of Neo-Classical Theism, it is clearly inconsistent with the God of Classical Theism. While there may be various other obstacles, this line of reasoning appears to uncover the most fundamental reasons why Buddhists cannot also be Classical Theists. But is this obstacle insurmountable?

---

[13] If you missed the lecture that day, we formulate Leibniz's Law of Identity in light of various of his texts, including a letter to de Volder, in which he writes, "... if you take two bodies, A and B, equal and with the same shape and motion, it will follow from such a notion of body ... that they have nothing by which they can be distinguished intrinsically. Is it therefore the case that A and B are not different individuals? Or is it possible that there are different things that cannot, in any way, be distinguished intrinsically? ... things that differ ought to differ in some way." Also see *The Monadology* section 9, "... there are never two beings in nature that are perfectly alike, two beings in which it is not possible to discover an internal difference, one founded on an intrinsic denomination." For a more in-depth discussion, see *Discourse on Metaphysics*, sections 8 and 9. Leibniz, 1989.

[14] In contrast to the Mahayana Buddhist tradition, the Abhidharma/Theravada tradition argues that dharmas, metaphysical building blocks that are akin to atoms, are not empty. On this view, atoms are taken to be basic or fundamental realties. See Westerhoff, 2018.

2.2 No-Thing Response

McNabb and Baldwin have argued that because God lacks properties altogether, God is metaphysically simple and so shouldn't be considered a thing or an object. Rather, God is the grounding of all things and objects (McNabb and Baldwin, 2022). As the Neo-Platonic tradition stresses, God is literally no-thing (Hart, 2014, p. 107). He is beyond existence altogether. But what do the metaphysical theses of Buddhism apply to? According to the experts we surveyed, they apply to things, objects, and phenomena. They *don't* apply to that which is beyond the realm of phenomenal existence and thinghood, should there be such a realm. And so, some Buddhists may be open to the possibility that there is such a realm of existence, for all we know. In fact, as we will show below, there are historical Buddhist traditions that seem to say just this. Because the central theses of Buddhism apply only to things, a Buddhist need not be compelled to apply the theses to the God of Classical Theism, who, recall, is not another existent. Thus, Buddhists who wants to be a theist can whole heartily endorse the aforementioned lines by Jay Garfield and endorse the existence of a God who is no-thing and beyond existence as well.

2.3 Skillful Means and Emptiness

Perhaps some of our Buddhist readers are not happy with the No-Thing response. One concern might be that the essential theses should be applied to being simpliciter or towards any purportedly transcendent reality. While there are many Buddhist traditions that advocate such an approach, one particularly influential school of thought that gives voice to this objection is that of the Kyoto School, so called because it originated in Kyoto Japan in the twentieth century. Elsewhere, Baldwin explicates the sort of Buddhist metaphysics that rules out any sort of transcendent reality, dubbing it the metaphysics of *śūnyatā*, for example, the metaphysics of emptiness (Baldwin, 2016). Emptiness is another name for the Buddhist doctrine of *Pratityasamutpada*, co-dependent origination. On this view, nothing exists as a self-subsisting or isolated substance but rather everything is ultimately entwined in a net of relationships that is always in flux.[15]

Masao Abe explicitly rejects the possibility of Buddhism being consistent with the existence of any sort of transcendent reality. He writes,

> Mahayana Buddhism insists that everything in this world is mutable, transient and subject to time and change ... [it] does not expound the existence of an immutable, eternal, transcendent, and real behind of beyond this world. There is nothing eternal, transcendent, and real behind or beyond this world. (Abe, 1997, p. 139)

---

[15] For more on this point, see, for instance, Yagi and Swidler, 1990, pp. 84, 86 and 97.

Abe goes on to explicate codependent origination as the rejection of both transcendence and immanence, as the view that "everything is dependent on something else without exception, nothing whatsoever in the universe being independent and self-existing" (Abe, 1997, p. 140). Śūnyatā, boundless, limitless, and without form, "best describes the nature of ultimate Reality" (Abe, 1997, pp. 139–141). Of course, McNabb and Baldwin could point out that dependent origination is still being applied only to things and God is no-thing, but nonetheless, capturing the spirit of what Abe is likely getting at, Abe is against Western-minded philosophers associating śūnyatā with the negation of Platonic Being. That is, codependent origination is not tantamount to Parmenidean relative non-being, the sort of non-being understood as the negation of Parmenidean being. Śūnyatā is prior to any distinction between relative being and non-being. According to Abe, actually existing being (which, roughly, we may take to be the sorts of things that we encounter in everyday experience) is simultaneously being and non-being in the sense that to be an existing thing A, A always contains an element of non-A in order to be A. Put another way, a thing A is what it is in virtue of the fact that it is also not-A. This may seem nonsensical, but Seiichi Yagi offers us a clever way of understanding the view in terms of what he calls front-structure. Imagine a wall W separating rooms A and B. Dub *a* the side of the wall that faces room A and dub *b* the side of the wall that faces room B. W both separates and joins rooms A and B because the respective front-structures of A and B, *a* and *b*, are also constitutive parts of W. In other words, *a*, the front structure of A, is *a* but also non-*a* because it is a constitutive part of *b*, and, naturally, *b*, the front structure of B, is *b* but also non-*b* because it is a constitutive part of *a*. Other examples of front-structure include a house garden (the border of the garden is a constative part of both the garden and the house) and living organisms in an ecosystem (the fish and the algae and bacteria in the tank live, depend on, and interact with each other dynamically) (Yagi and Swidler, 1990, pp. 77–78; 85–86). Fish and algae in their ecosystems and rooms that share walls are illustrations of co-dependent origination; reflection on these and other examples reveals the way in which things are what they are but only because they are intertwined with things that they are not.

Generalizing this point at the highest level, Abe maintains that both being and non-being are conditioned. That is, neither has ontological priority over the other because both depend on something else, namely, the ultimate nonconditioned, or Śūnyatā. Abe writes, 'Śūnyatā is realized not only by negating the 'eternalist' view [Parmenidean being] but also by negating the 'nihilistic' view

[Parmenidean non-being]" (Abe, 1985, p. 127). The emptiness of śūnyatā is absolute non-being, or Absolute Nothingness, the negation of both being and non-being.

If Abe is correct, Mahayana Buddhism seems incompatible with Classical Theism. How are we to respond to this objection? Should we concede that Mahayana Buddhism is inconsistent with theism? For those who accept Abe's explication of śūnyatā as absolute nothingness, Classical Theism isn't a viable option. But it may well be that other strands of Buddhism that accept a different metaphysics may yet be shown to be consistent with Classical Theism. And perhaps there are some branches of Mahayana Buddhism that don't explicate śūnyatā the way that Abe does. For the time being, for sake of argument, suppose that Abe's metaphysical understanding of śūnyatā is correct, in the sense that this metaphysic is the one that is closest to the one taught in the Buddhist sutras, and so on. To reconcile this Buddhist teaching with Classical Theism, one might appeal to the Buddhist hermeneutic known as upāya, or skillful means. The skillful means hermeneutic technique was developed to help contemporary Buddhists make sense of how new theological developments could be made consistent with its original teachings.[16] The idea is that previous teachings may be seen as purely expedient, as useful means for attaining enlightenment. In a way analogous to how a science teacher may state half-truths and analogies to enable her student to understand physics, previous Buddhist teachings may consist of analogies and half-truths with the aim of helping Buddhists reach enlightenment. For example, Zen Buddhists reject traditional forms of mediation and methods of reaching enlightenment. The Rinzai school maintains that reflection on kōans, riddles or puzzles that have no apparent rational resolution, can lead one to break through the illusion of ego and thereby achieve enlightenment. According to the Sōtō school, founded by Dōgen, 'just sitting' can likewise lead to enlightenment. For radical iconoclasts in the Zen tradition, any teaching or practice that enables one to achieve nirvāṇa is enough.

While other modern-day Mahayana Buddhists might not go as far as Zen Buddhists, they may be inclined to modify certain Buddhist teachings. They may be motivated to argue that the impermanence and interdependence theses need not be applied to that which is beyond existence, even if Buddhism as it was originally taught did. One might think that, perhaps, if the Buddha taught there was a reality beyond the realm of existence (i.e., Brahman or God), it

---

[16] We discuss the skillful means hermeneutic in more detail in McNabb and Baldwin, 2024, pp. 89–90.

would have prevented his followers from possessing right realization. Maybe Buddha's disciples would have believed that God was merely an object among other objects. Nonetheless, as humanity matures and philosophy develops, we can explain that the original teachings were given to specific people at specific times. Being more mature, we can now understand that the application of the Buddha's central metaphysical theses has applications that are limited in scope. This route would show that there is conceptual room for a Buddhist to affirm that the realm of existents is empty of own being (this would correspond to the mode of existence proper to things on Classical Theism) and yet, also affirm the reality of that which is not empty (which would correspond to the mode of the being proper to God on Classical Theism).

Perhaps the reader now will concede that, perhaps, some form Buddhism could be (or at least reasonably considered to be) consistent with theism. That'd be interesting progress, but the main problem would remain unsolved. Really, when we want to know whether the metaphysics of Buddhism are consistent with theism, we want to know whether there are actual Buddhist traditions which are consistent with and even support theistic belief or something rather like it. Are there important Buddhist thinkers who thought that while the realm of things is empty of own nature, there is still that which is not empty of own nature? We argue that, yes, there is such a tradition.

2.4 Shentong versus Rangtong

When analytic philosophers hear about the doctrine of emptiness, they typically interpret it through a non-neutral theological lens. To be empty, one must lack own being. But this isn't the only way to understand emptiness. As Michael Sheehy and Klaus Mathes point out, '... the general reader of English literature on Buddhism may not be aware that such an understanding of emptiness reflects a particular interpretation of it, advanced by Sakya, Kadam, and Geluk orders ... In Tibetan discourse this position is referred to as rangtong' (Sheehy and Mathes, 2019, p. 1). However, there is another position known as Shentong, which, due its suppression by the fifth Dalai Lama, isn't well-known. The Shentong tradition, especially seen through the Jonang school, argues that there is another conception of emptiness that is preferable to the rangtong position. On this view, reality can be empty of other but still not be empty of own being. Philosophers like Dölpopa (1292–1361 AD) and Tāranātha (1575–1635) would go on to argue, largely inspired by the Buddha sutras (*Tathāgatagarbha sutras*), that there can't be impermanent and interdependent phenomena without that which is permanent and independent (Sheehy and Mathes, 2019, p. 3).

> If the permanent were negated, the impermanent would be negated. If there were no Buddha, there would be no sentient beings. If there were no primordial awareness, there would be no consciousness ... That which is the primordial awareness of the basic space of phenomena is permanent, unconditioned primordial awareness ... beyond simile ... immutable, fully established ... great bliss. (Dölpopa 2010, pp. 153–154)

Dölpopa would call this permanent reality, the Buddha nature; the Buddha nature is primordial awareness and pure bliss (Dölpopa, 2010, pp. 153–154). He even goes on to call the Buddha-nature omnipotent, omniscient, and transcendent (Dölpopa, 2010, pp. 153–154). Speaking of permanent reality, in Tāranātha's *Twenty-One Differences*, Tāranātha has Dölpopa say, 'that it can be taken to be beyond both an entity/existence and a nonentity/nonexistence.' (Mathes, 2004, pp. 285–328) Ultimate reality is not a thing, nor is it empty of own being, but there are things and all of them are empty of own being. What is stated here should sound familiar, both to readers of Classical Theism and Neo-Platonism more generally (McNabb, forthcoming).

Dölpopa isn't the only medieval Buddhist philosopher to think there is permanent reality. In Japan around the same time, Shinran Shonin (1173–1263) emerged arguing that the supreme *nirvāṇa* is the uncreated, true, and a nondual reality; it is eternal bliss (Shinran, 1997, p. 153). Elsewhere he calls supreme *nirvāṇa* the Buddha nature and clarifies that it pervades all sentient beings (Shinran, 1997, p. 99). Now, one might be tempted to take Shinran's claims to entail that Buddha nature is utterly impersonal and devoid of personal traits. Yet, there is a reason to think that this isn't the case. Shinran says that the Amida Buddha 'comes forth' from supreme Nirvana (Shinran,1997, p. 50). Amida Buddha in the Pure Land tradition is an individual that one can place their trust in, in order to be reborn in a pure land in the next life. Amida Buddha, being a person, has personal qualities. Yet, it is proper to say that the Amida Buddha is otherwordly in his true nature. In fact, he is beyond 'existence and non-existence' (Hirota, 1997, p. 59). This story isn't too different from what Christianity teaches. Namely, that God is a nondual reality that pervades and grounds all, and yet, took on a human nature. Those who call on this reality for salvation can be saved. Once again, you have a ground of all being, the Buddha nature. The Buddha nature is eternal bliss, non-dual, and can in someway, manifest itself as a person. Something was in the Buddhist water. Classical theism isn't far off, if off at all.[17]

---

[17] One reviewer suggested that Chan Buddhism is in a similar position to Shentong with respect to being an analog for Classical Theism. The *Platform Sutra* argues that original nature is inherently pure and unshaken. It's been suggested to us that we could interpret this to mean that pure nature is simple and immutable. See Hua, 2014.

Now, James Rooney has recently developed his own model for how the Mahayana tradition more generally can be rendered consistent with Trinitarianism. The idea being that since each member of the Godhead, the Father, the Son and the Holy Spirit, is dependent on each other, the Godhead itself is empty (Rooney, forthcoming). Rooney develops a novel and ingenious model of reconciliation. There is a sense in which even God is empty, and yet, we can still think God is *a se*. However, there is the worry that his view cannot make sense of how all things could be 'impermanent.' One response Rooney gives to this problem is to argue that even though *nirvāṇa* is beyond being and non-being it is permanent. But if Buddhists can make this move to avoid the problem, why can't Classical Theists say that God is beyond being and non-being so the metaphysical theses in question don't apply to God? Perhaps Rooney's way of making Trinitarianism consistent with the Mahayana tradition and the view we've sketched out here, are complimentary accounts. We propose that God is empty of own being in the sense that each person of the Trinity depends on each of the others but God is not empty in the sense that God depends on another for His being. To put the point another way, we propose that in one sense, Godhead, the essence of the divine being, is the ground and source of all being, and so has own being. But in another sense, insofar as each person of the triune Godhead, Father, Son and Holy Spirit, depends on each of the others, Godhead lacks own being. Nonetheless, Rooney worries that our approach really only gets us to panentheism at best (Rooney forthcoming). Elsewhere, McNabb has argued that the metaphysics assumed in Shentong Buddhism and Shankara's Advaita Vedānta tradition can be rendered consistent with Classical Theism (McNabb, forthcoming). This will be explored more below.

Let's go back to the Shentong tradition. If our argument is successful, then there is at least one Buddhist tradition such that its central metaphysics are consistent with the central metaphysics of Classical Theism. But one might object that all we've shown is that the Shentong tradition is an aberrant or abnormal tradition. The upshot is that rather than supporting our view that Buddhism and Classical Theism are consistent, we've at best shown that we should view the Shentong tradition as a heretical offshoot of Buddhism. Truly orthodox Buddhist traditions explicitly deny or otherwise leave no room for a transcendent or permanent reality. It is to this next objection that we now turn.

2.5 Smells Like Nirvana

There are texts which Buddhists can and have appealed to which discuss that which is permanent. Keith Ward has argued convincingly that *The*

Dhammapada describes *nirvāṇa* in this way (Ward, 1994, pp. 163–167). As Ward points out, *nirvāṇa* is said to be peaceful as well as infinite joy.[18] Ward seems to think there are hermeneutical reasons to interpret *nirvāṇa* as pure bliss or consciousness (Ward, 1994, pp. 163–167). Verse 202 states that 'There is no ill like the aggregates. And no bliss higher than peace (Nibbana).' The next verse describes *nirvāṇa* as 'the highest bliss.' Verse 218 then states that 'One who is intent upon the ineffable (Nibbana), dwells with mind inspired, and is not bound by sense pleasures – such a man is called 'One Bound Upstream.'" *Nirvāṇa* is described as unknowable. In verse 383, we see that 'Knowing the destruction of all conditioned things, become, oh holy man, the knower of the uncreate (Nibbana).'[19] To summarize: *Nirvāṇa* is unknowable and uncreated, and yet, it is considered the highest bliss and peaceful. The aforementioned verses seem to support the view that at least for some Buddhist traditions, permanence has a place.

But one might object that this view is implausible on the grounds that *nirvāṇa* literally translates to 'blowing out.' Continuing, one might argue that *The Dhammapada* only discusses *nirvāṇa* in a positive way (e.g., pure bliss), as a skillful means (*upaya*), an aid to help readers reach and want to reach enlightenment. In reality there is nothing to *nirvāṇa*. Along these lines, we should interpret any passages that present *nirvāṇa* in any positive way, reductively; we ought to maintain that *nirvāṇa* is simply the lack of suffering that is achieved by the enlightened when there is a cessation of desire and the cessation of rebirth.

This is one way to interpret *nirvāṇa*. But we don't find the evidence for this interpretation to be overwhelming. As Thanissaro Bhikku points out, in Buddha's Indian culture, a fire ceasing to be does not actually entail that it no longer exists in any sense (Thanissaro, 1993, pp. 15–38). In ancient India, if fire was extinguished, it was still alive and potent.

> As fire through loss of fuel
> Grows still [extinguished] in its own source,
> So thought by loss of activeness
> Grows still in its own source.[20]

And the Buddha seems to use fire language not to describe ceasing to be, but to describe that the unboundedness is indescribable.[21] As Thanissaro puts it:

---

[18] I (Tyler McNabb) point this out in McNabb, 2024, pp. 46–53.
[19] Following verses can be found in *Dhammapada*, translated by A. Buddharakkhita (Kandy: Buddhist Publication Society, 1985).
[20] Here we are indebted to Thanissaro Bhikku's translation of MaiU 6.34 on page 20.
[21] See especially *Middle Length Discourses*, chapter 72.

> The image of an extinguished fire carried no connotations of annihilation for the early Buddhists. Rather, the aspects of the fire that to them had significance for the mind-fire analogy are these: Fire, when burning, is in a state of agitation, dependence, attachment, and entrapment-both clinging and being stuck to its sustenance. Extinguished, it becomes calm, independent, indeterminate, and unattached. (Thanissaro, 2016, p. 42)

Thanissaro proposes that instead of interpreting *nirvāṇa* to mean 'ceasing to be,' we should interpret it in a way related to freedom and liberation. In fact, Thanissaro even interprets the Buddha as not denying the existence of the self. In the Buddha's *Connected Discourses* (*Samyutta Nikaya*), Vacchagotta approaches the Buddha and asks the Buddha if there is a self. The Buddha, instead of answering, simply remains silent.[22] Ānanda, his disciple, became perplexed and asked why his teacher didn't give Vacchagotta an answer. The Buddha replied:

> "If, Ānanda, when I was asked by the wanderer Vacchagotta, 'Is there a self?' I had answered, 'There is a self,' this would have been siding with those ascetics and brahmins who are eternalists. And if, when I was asked by him, 'Is there no self?' I had answered, 'There is no self,' this would have been siding with those ascetics and brahmins who are annihilationists.
>
> "If, Ānanda, when I was asked by the wanderer Vacchagotta, 'Is there a self?' I had answered, 'There is a self,' would this have been consistent on my part with the arising of the knowledge that 'all phenomena are nonself'?"

"No, venerable sir."

> "And if, when I was asked by him, 'Is there no self?' I had answered, 'There is no self,' the wanderer Vacchagotta, already confused, would have fallen into even greater confusion, thinking, 'It seems that the self I formerly had does not exist now.'"[23]

These texts go to show that the Buddha doesn't actually endorse that there is no self. Instead, he argues that if he said there was a self, that wouldn't be consistent with the view that all phenomena are empty. And if he said there was no self, he would have been siding with the annihilationists, whom he didn't agree with. There is a third reason mentioned for why the Buddha remained silent. If he were to answer that there was no self, it would have brought greater confusion to Vacchagotta. As Thanissaro mentions, elsewhere, the Buddha argues that in order to achieve enlightenment, we need to not have a view of the self.[24] It might be the case that there is a self or something like a self, but yet,

---

[22] See *Connected Discourses* 44:10.
[23] This passage is from Trl. Bhikkhu Boddi, *Connected Discourses*, 44:10 (Somerville Wisdom Publications, 2000) 1393–1395.
[24] cf. Linked Discourse, 5:15.

it is better, at least for his time and disciples, to have no view of it whatsoever so that there won't be confusion. The Buddha often stressed agnosticism on big metaphysical questions. This is why there were early Indian Buddhist traditions which endorsed the existence of a self (Thanissaro, 1993, p. 91).[25]

We are now in a place where we can summarize what we've argued for thus far. We've argued that Classical Theism denies that God is a thing and, therefore, that Buddhist metaphysical theses that apply to things would not apply to God. It follows that Classical Theism is consistent with Buddhism. Second, we argued that if one thought the Buddhist's metaphysical theses originally applied to even that which is beyond existence, the Buddhist can now restrict the theses using a skillful means hermeneutic. We then engaged an objection to our argument that we need to show that an actual Buddhist tradition is consistent with Buddhism. We responded by explicating the Shentong tradition and its endorsement of there being the permanent and independent Buddha nature. Finally, we argued that the Shentong tradition shouldn't be seen as heretical, simply because it endorses that which is permanent, as there are good textual reasons to interpret *nirvāṇa* much in the same way. Having now explored to what extent the central metaphysical theses of Buddhism are consistent with Classical Theism, we stay in India to discuss to what extent Hinduism(s) can be seen as consistent with Classical Theism.

3 Hinduism and Classical Theism

3.1 Hinduism(s)

Surveying the relevant metaphysics of Hinduism is more challenging than surveying other Eastern traditions. In part, the reason relates to whether 'Hinduism' refers to a unique religious tradition or if the term is a mere a fiction (mis)used by scholars to incongruently group different Indian religions together. Jessica Frazier, in her *Hindu Worldviews*, understands Hinduism to relate to those traditions that take *The Vedas*, *The Upanishads*, and various *Sutras* as Scripture (Frazier, 2017, p. 20). There is no singular, monolithic Hindu worldview, however. There really are different Hinduisms, each containing its own unique set of metaphysical principles. There are schools within schools of each tradition. Primary traditions within Hinduism include *Nyāya*, *Vaiśeṣika*, *Sāṅkhya*, *Yoga*, *Pūrvamīmāṃsā*, and *Vedānta*. Within those broader traditions there are even narrower traditions. For example, within Vedānta there is the Dvaita tradition, where there are three types of entities that exist: God,

---

[25] See Leonard Priestly, "Pudgalavada Buddhist Philosophy." Internet Enclyopedia of Philosophy, https://iep.utm.edu/pudgalavada-buddhist-philosophy/. See also McNabb's discussion of it in McNabb, 2024.

creaturely souls, and inanimate objects (Stoker, *IEP*). Liberation relates largely to devotion to God. This contrasts with the Advaita tradition, where at the fundamental level, all is the impersonal Brahman. The former endorses a standard theistic metaphysical picture, while the latter is typically understood to be a textbook example of monism.

As you can see, it is well beyond this Element to argue that each Hindu tradition is consistent with Classical Theism. Though it seems rather obvious that there are Hindu traditions which are not at least prima facie consistent with Classical Theism. Generally, Shankara's interpretation of the Advaita tradition is seen as a tradition that is in competition with Classical Theism because it adheres to metaphysics that are simply not reconcilable with the metaphysics of Classical Theism. On the contrary, in this section, we will argue that Advaita Vedānta can be interpreted in a way that it is consistent with Classical Theism. We first, however, further explicate the tradition.

3.2 Advaita Vedānta

Victoria Harrison summarizes the Advaita picture of reality well:

> *Layer 1: Absolute reality*
> Nirguna, Brahman, Qualityless Brahman, Brahman/Ātman.
> *Layer 2:*
> *Absolute reality seen through categories imposed by human thought* Saguna Brahman, Brahman with qualities. Creator and governor of the world and a personal god (Īśvara, or Iswara).
> *Layer 3:*
> *Conventional reality.* (Harrison, 2013, p. 58)

The idea is that there is a level of existence, call it the conventional level of existence, where middle-sized objects and a personal God exist. That is, we can talk about iPhones, PS5s, and Dr. Pepper bottles existing. However, more fundamental to this reality is seeing that Brahman is the fundamental reality on which all other realities depend. However, Brahman seen in this way is still conceptualized subjectively in accord with human categories as though it were a personal reality. At the most fundamental level of reality, however, the enlightened mind sees that all reality is the propertyless and impersonal Brahman. As Christopher Isherwood and Swami Prabhavananda put it, 'Are there then two Gods-one the impersonal Brahaman, the other the personal Iswara? No ... God the person is not the ultimate nature of Brahman' (Isherwood and Prabavananda, 1975, p. 18).

What's at the heart of the Advaita tradition is prioritizing certain *Upanishads* that express that, fundamentally, there is only Brahman.

Eastern Philosophy and Classical Theism

> You remember that truth and Self are one ... You are That! (Shree Swami and Yeats, 2003, p. 104)

> The Self brings everything, for thereby everything is known. He is the footprint that brings a man to his goal ... The Self is nearer than all else; dearer than son, dearer than wealth, dearer than anything ... for the Self is God. (Shree Swami and Yeats, 2003, p. 119)

Passages like these inspired Shankara[26] to argue the following:

> Brahman is the reality-the one existence, absolutely independent of human thought or idea. Because of the ignorance of our human minds, the universe seems to be composed of diverse forms. It is Brahman alone. A jar made for clay is not other than clay. The form of the jar has no independent existence. What, then is the jar? Merely an invented name! The form of the jar can never be perceived apart from the clay ... The reality is the clay itself. (Shankara, 1975, p. 70)

Again, for Shankara, Brahaman is the substratum of the self, and yet, transcends all forms (Shankaracharya, 1938, p. 23). Brahman both appears somehow wholly immanent and wholly transcendent. But because God is so immanent, 'There exists no other material cause of this phenomenal universe except Brahman. Hence this whole universe is 'But Brahman and nothing else' (Shankaracharya, 1938, pp. 26–27). We are told that a pot is never different from the earth which it is made (Shankaracharya, 1938, p. 37). The Universe does not exist apart from the Atman. Our perception of it as having an independent existence is false, like our perception of the blueness in the sky. How can a superimposed attribute have any existence, apart from its substratum? (Shankara, 1975, p. 71)

But supposedly, Shankara doesn't have room for multiplicity of any sort. There is no plurality for existence; there is only Brahman. Shankara endorses an impersonal pantheistic God, not the God of Classical Theism, or so it is argued (Tennent, 2002, p. 42). In the following section we challenge this common conception.

3.3 An Interpretation and Synthesis

We don't think the radical monist interpretation is the best interpretation of Shankara, even though we've appealed to it elsewhere (Baldwin and McNabb, 2018). Before we address this, however, we want to make clear the commonality that exists between Classical Theism and the Advaita Tradition. In another work, Shankara states that fundamental existence is without an attribute and free from being moved upon altogether (Shankaracharya, 1938, p. 17). Notice here, Shankara seems to affirm that God is without attribute or is propertyless. Recall

---

[26] By Shankara, we just mean the author or authors of the works associated with his name.

again that Classical Theists of the stripe we have in mind also think God is propertyless, at least univocally speaking. Keith Ward also recognizes that both Thomas Aquinas and Shankara seem to be on the same page about the doctrine of simplicity as he states, 'The deep unity of these views should be clear' (Ward, 1994, p. 147). Notice, also, that Brahman is immovable, so He is impassible. Elsewhere, Shankara states that 'Brahman is supreme. He is the reality-the one without a second. He is pure consciousness, free from any taint. He is tranquility itself. He has neither beginning nor end. He does not change. He is joy for ever. He transcends the appearance of the manifold ...' (Shankara, 1975, p. 71). Attentive readers might recognize that Dölpopa's claim that the Buddha nature is pure bliss and primordial awareness seems to also echo Shankara here.

But what about the differences? Isn't Brahman impersonal, while Classical Theists think, at least analogically, that God is personal? Ward thinks the conflict is only skin deep as he says, 'it may be more appropriate ... to regard such formulations as faltering attempts to express things that cannot be adequately described in available human concepts at all' (Ward, 1994, p. 153). We think the Classical Theist can argue that God cannot be said to be personal or impersonal in a univocal sense. We can only say that He is personal and impersonal by way of analogy. So, there is some sense in which we can say God is impersonal and another sense in which we can say He is personal. Conflict isn't necessary.

Supposing the argument so far is successful, pressing problems remain. Advaita endorses a nondualistic metaphysic, whereas Classical Theists are metaphysical dualists. Daniel Soars has recently argued for a synthesis of sorts, between Thomas Aquinas and Shanakra (Soars, 2023). That is, he argues that Aquinas shouldn't be seen as endorsing dualism as such since, for Aquinas, as we've stated before, God is not simply an object among other objects. Rather, He is what makes objects possible. In other words, as we've also stated before, God isn't a being but is rather the ground of all beings. Because of this, it would be misleading to say that Classical Theism, at least of this Thomistic stripe we've embraced, must endorse a dualistic metaphysic. Whatever else the theory amounts to, a dualistic metaphysics proposes, at root, that there are two kinds of things or objects. But if we can't take God to be an object, then we can't very well set in contrast the being of God with the being of things and say we have two kinds of things or objects. Since God is not an object or thing, we need not endorse dualism.

Anantanand Rambachan argues that there is even room for 'manyness' in the Advaita tradition (Rambachan, 2015, p. 13). In fact, in personal correspondence, we asked Rambachan if one could say that objects exist insofar as they participate in Brahman. He replied, 'Your language of participation is an interesting possibility, if by participation you mean that nothing exists apart from brahman, nothing exists independently of brahman, and while things may have unique attributes, etc., at the most fundamental level of being or existence, all is brahman' (Anatanand Rambachan, *Personal Correspondence*, 2023). Of course, Classical Theists will be very inclined to agree with the relevant stipulations. Ward also thinks there is room for manyness in Shankara as he states the following:

> What is the status of the individual mind, the agent and en-joyer, which we regard as the human soul? Sankara says, 'The Self does not exist ... as an agent and enjoyer ... the qualities of mind ... are wrongly superimposed upon the Self.' But then it follows that the individual soul is in a very important respect not identical with Brahman. (Ward, 1994, p. 151)

But what are we to make of claim that the jar made of clay does not exist? Well, there is some sense in which Classical Theists have even stated that only God is and humans are not. Brian Davies makes the point in the following:

> God is the ultimate reality. And Catherine of Sienna, whose thinking is governed by the notion of God as the source of everything, repeatedly says that only God is and she herself is not. In similar vein, [Jonathan] Edwards explains that creatures are, in a sense, 'empty'. By creature being thus wholly and universally dependent on God', writes Edwards, 'it appears that the creature is nothing, and that God is all'. (Davies, 2003, p. 373)

Humans, recall, only exist in a participatory sense. They exist but not in the same way that God exists. Really there is only clay, or in this case, God.

At this stage of the argument, we hope to have convinced the reader that Shankara's views can be interpreted through Classical Theist lenses. Even so, there is one final problem to deal with. Shankara does in fact say that the material cause of the universe is God and that ultimately, 'I am Brahmin.' Surely, this is not reconcilable with Classical Theism. We think even this conclusion is too quick. While Shankara makes claims about Brahman being the material cause of the world, he also, quoting *The Bhagavad Gita*, says, '... all creatures exist within me. I do not mean that they exist within me physically. That is my divine mystery' (Shankara, 1975, pp. 70–71). So, Shankara is *not* endorsing that God has a body and it is identical with the physical universe. It's rather mysterious how it is that creatures exist in God. But, on Shankara's view, we can say that God is the material cause of the universe in the sense that nothing exists apart from Him. Moreover, we can say that behind our existence is God's existence. There's no need to read his claim that God is the material cause of things to mean anything more. Utilizing the doctrine of analogy, we can say that God is not univocally the material cause of the universe but that He is analogically the material cause of the universe. Making this move, we think we have made a plausible case for the view that Shankara's Advaita tradition can be read so that it is logically consistent with the metaphysics of Classical Theism. We are now in the position to leave India and go further East.

4 Early China, Confucianism, and Classical Theism

4.1 China and the Transcendent

Having worked in China for a few years, I (Tyler) heard on more than one occasion that 'the Chinese don't believe in God.' The idea expressed to me was that the Chinese people are very different from Westerners, that the Chinese never believed in God. Westerners might claim to see 'God's fingerprint' in nature but the Chinese, on the whole, do not. Chinese academics, not unlike certain Western counterparts, in order to explain and account for religious belief and practice, typically assume that religion is purely a sociological phenomenon. Differences in the sociological makeup and histories account for the fact that the idea of God is largely absent in the East and why it is so prevalent in the West. As Chun-Fang Yu puts it plainly, 'there is no God transcendent separate from the world and there is no heaven outside of the universe to which human beings would want to go for refuge' (Yu, 2007). Roger Ames approvingly summarizes Joseph Needham's work as he says his work 'dissociates early Chinese cosmology from such familiar assumptions frightened in our own narrative about some external and thus objective source of cosmic order ... "Chinese ideals involved neither God nor Law"' (Ames, 2011, p. 211). For Needham, there is no need for a transcendent grounding of meaning or morality. In his own work, Ames plays down the role of teleology and god in Chinese culture more generally (Ames, 2011, p. 211). Likewise, the famous French Sinologist Marcel Granet argues that 'Chinese wisdom has no need of the idea of God' (Granet, 1934, p. 279). After discussing how Chinese officials see the need to Confucianize the atheistic Communist Party of China, Fenggand Yang says that it is believed that 'Confucianism is the best spiritual foundation for practical solutions of the major social and political problems of China today ... it can withstand the imperialistic or expansionist Christian civilization of the West' (Yang, 2016, p. 30). Confucianism in today's China is seen as an alternative to Christianity. Christianity believes in a personal God, whereas Confucianism believes in human nature. While Christianity believes in an objective and transcendent law, Confucianism believes in the structure of community. We need to reject the former and believe the latter.

4.2 The Analects

Scholars will often appeal to *The Analects* as evidence that Confucius was not a theist, and then derive a normative claim from the relevant passage about what Confucians should believe about God.[27] Of course, the author of *The Analects* never comes out and says that God does not exist, or that there is no heaven above us or hell below us. Instead, scholars usually appeal to *Analects* 6:22, where the author states we should, 'Respect the spirits but keep them at a distance.' The idea is that Confucius didn't actually believe in the spirits for, if he did, he wouldn't tell us to keep them at a distance. Instead, he was a quasi-naturalist who wanted to gradually lead his audience away from believing in the supernatural. Hall and Ames argue that Confucius wanted us to have a 'respectful detachment' of the supernatural (Hall and Ames, 1987, p. 196).

There are reasons, however, not to take *Analects* 6:22 as evidence for Confucius being a naturalist. Following Herrlee Creel, Kelly James and Justin Winslett point out that in *Analects* 16:15, Confucius informs the reader that a person keeps his son at a distance (Kelly and Winslett, 2023, p. 63).[28] Obviously, Confucius isn't arguing that a father should deny their son's existence or even have no relationship with their son. Appealing to *Analects* 6:22 as evidence for Confucius' atheism seems a bit premature.

Really, answering the question of whether Confucius was a theist (or something near about) relates to studying the concept of heaven (*Tian*, 天) in the *Analects*. Eric Cline puts it like this:

> Along the spectrum of views we have been examining, the strongest claims about the continuity or discontinuity between Western monotheistic views and Kongzi's [Confucius'] view stem from passages concerning *Tian*. The concept of *Tian* is historically related to some of the earliest conceptions of a supreme deity in China, including Shangdi, who existed alongside various ancestral and nature spirits. Those who defend a monotheistic interpretation of *Tian* tend to view Shangdi and *Tian* as the same idea, which supports their interpretation of *Tian* as a theistic concept. (Cline, 2021, pp. 76–121)

Ames and Rosemont seem to think that *Tian* should be interpreted in naturalist friendly way such that it is simply the world (Ames and Rosemont, 1999, p. 47). Cline though finds this problematic as they 'do not cite any passages from the *Analects* in support of their claims,' and this is 'a particularly pressing problem because ... there are a number of passages in the Analects in which *Tian* is described as an agent that acts in the world—not as the world itself' (Cline, 2021, pp. 76–121). Elsewhere, Hall and Ames state that *Tian* in the *Analects* is

---

[27] Here, we use "Confucius" as a stand-in for "author or authors of *The Analects*."
[28] cf. Creel, 1932, pp. 55–99.

not analogous to God because of how *Tian* is "unqualifiedly immanent" (Hall and Ames, 1987, p. 206). Like Ames and Rosemont, Philip Ivanhoe rejects that *Tian* could be read interchangeably with 'God.' Though for Ivanhoe, *Tian* nonetheless is 'an impersonal yet concerned agent and a force for human good' (Ivanhoe 2007, p. 213).

Contrasting these opinions, James Legge states that *Tian* 'has had much of the force of the name Jahve, as explained by God Himself to Moses' (Legge, 1881, pp. 10–11).[29] Benjamin Schwartz similarly states, 'If there is any central religious term in the *Analects*, it is the term "heaven" and here again Confucius is to a degree a transmitter ... Heaven above all is the source of the moral order' (Schwartz, 1985, p. 122).[30] So what does the *Analects* say about *Tian*? It says that Heaven is what leaders model themselves after:

> The Master said, "How great was Yao as a ruler? So majestic! It is Heaven that is great, and it was Yao who modeled himself upon it. So vast! Among the common people there were none who were able to find words to describe him. How majestic in his accomplishments, and glorious in cultural splendor. (*Analects* 8:19)[31]

Tian is what enables humans to have virtue:

> The Master said, 'It is Heaven itself that has endowed me with virtue. What have I to fear from the likes of Huan Tui? (*Analects* 7:23)

And of course, when we are not on our best behavior, *Tian* can punish us:

> If I have done anything wrong, may Heaven punish me. (*Analects* 6:28)

Tian is also said to have laws (*Analects* 8:16) and perhaps knows Confucius himself (*Analects* 14:35)! So, *Tian* can be read as the grounding of goodness itself. It is the gifter of virtue and the punisher of the unjust. This is why people like Robert Endo state that it 'is a teleological force' and 'final cause,' of humanity (Eno, 1990, pp. 165; 121).

4.3 The *Mencius*

But how was Confucius received? Perhaps we could learn how best to interpret Confucius through reading his, chronologically speaking, nearby interpreters. Part of the Confucian canon is the work titled *Mencius*, ascribed to Mencius of

---

[29] For a more recent theistic-friendly interpretation of Confucius and *Tian*, see also Slingerland, 2006. He states, "Heaven possessed all of the powers of the Lord on High and in addition had the ability to charge a representative on earth with the Mandate to rule." See xviii.
[30] Cf., Clark and Winslett, 2023, p. 58.
[31] References from the *Analects* are taken from Slingerland, 2006.

the Zhou dynasty. Mencius uses the *Shijing* to say that *Tian* created humanity and gives us our moral natures:

> Mencius said, "One's natural tendencies enable one to do good; this is what I mean by human nature being good. When one does what is not good, it is not the fault of one's native capacities. The mind of pity and commiseration is possessed by all human beings; the mind of shame and dislike is possessed by all human beings; the mind of respectfulness and reverence is possessed by all human beings; and the mind that knows right and wrong is possessed by all human beings. The mind of pity and commiseration is humaneness; the mind of shame and dislike is rightness; the mind of respectfulness and reverence is propriety; and the mind that knows right and wrong is wisdom. Humaneness, rightness, propriety, and wisdom are not infused into us from without. We definitely possess them. It is just that we do not think about it, that is all. Therefore it is said, "Seek and you will get it; let go and you will lose it." That some differ from others by as much as twice, or five times, or an incalculable order of magnitude is because there are those who are unable fully to develop their capacities. The ode says, Heaven, in giving birth to humankind, Created for each thing its own rule. The people's common disposition Is to love this admirable Virtue.[32] (Mencius 6A6.1–2)

As Joshua Brown points out (Brown, 2024, p. 45), *Tian* is also said to be the providential guiding force:

> Wan Zhang asked, "Some people say that Yu's Virtue was weak and he did not transmit the power to rule to someone worthy but rather to his own son. Is this true?"
> Mencius said, "No, that is not true. When Heaven gave the power to rule to the worthiest, it was given to the worthiest. When Heaven gave it to a son, it was given to a son. Shun presented Yu to Heaven. Seventeen years passed, and Shun died. At the end of three years' mourning, Yu to *Tian* and after seventeen years, Shun died. At the end of three years' mourning, Yu withdrew from Shun's son to Yangcheng. The people of the realm followed Yu. It was as it was after Yao died and they did not follow Yao's son but followed Shun. Yu presented his minister, Yi, to Heaven, and after seven years, Yu died. At the end of the three years' mourning, Yi withdrew from Yu's son to the north of Mount Qi. Those going for an audience at court and those engaged in litigation did not follow Yi but followed Yu's son, Qi. They said, "This is the son of our ruler." The singers did not sing about Yi but sang about Qi, saying, "This is the son of our ruler." "Danzhu was not equal to his father, and Shun's son was also not equal to his father. Shun assisted Yao, and Yu assisted Shun, and as this went on over the course of years, they conveyed rich benefits upon the people over a long period of time. Qi was worthy and able reverently to continue the Way of Yu. Yi had assisted Yu for

---

[32] References to Mencius are taken from, Mencius, *Mencius*, trl. Irene Bloom (New York: Colombia University Press, 2009).

only a few years, and he had not been able to confer rich benefits upon the people for a long period of time. Shun and Yu differed from Yi in their periods of service, and their sons differed greatly in their worthiness. All this was owing to Heaven and was not something that could be brought about by human beings. (Mencius 5A6.1–2)

Further, Brown points out that for Mencius, Heaven confers offices upon men in 6B3.5 (Brown, 2024, p. 59).

And as with Confucius, Brown appeals to 6A1.6, to show that in *Mencius*, *Tian* is seen as the exemplar and source of goodness (Brown, 2024, p. 45). Brown argues that naturalizing *Tian* simply cannot make sense of the doctrine of the Mandate of Heaven,[33] nor can it make sense of how *Tian* is used in *Mencius* (Brown, 2024, p. 44).

4.4 Cognitive Science of Religion and China

Clark and Winslett devote a chapter detailing how the paradigm view in cognitive science of religion is that belief in the supernatural is an evolutionary spandrel (Clark and Winslett, 2023, pp. 139–162). There are various stories one can tell but perhaps the story that gets the most attention goes something like this:

> Belief in God is the result of having a hypersensitive agency detection device (HADD). Humans sense agents, even when they are not there. An organism that senses agency a bit more than she should, will be better off surviving than an organism that doesn't sense agency enough. Nonetheless, the sensitivity to detecting agency creates in us, a perception of seeing a transcendent 'fingerprint' when humans look out into nature. (cf. Barrett, 2011)

Throw in an inbuilt theory of mind and a natural tendency to see teleology in nature, and we have a plausible case for why humans naturally believe in the supernatural. *Contra* the 'religion is purely sociological' view discussed earlier, religion is natural to human faculties. And the Chinese, on average, detect agency and teleology in similar ways as their western counterparts (Hornbeck et al., 2017). If theism was prevalent in the Zhou Dynasty, and cognitive science tells us that humans are natural supernaturalists, then why should we interpret Confucius and Mencius through twenty-first-century naturalistic lenses? (Clark and Winslett 2023, pp. 139–162). Why not interpret *Tian* as something more than the physical world? Let's say you aren't convinced that Confucius was a theist but rather you think that it is undetermined. Nonetheless, recall that our

---

[33] The mandate of heaven is a popular concept in Chinese political philosophy where the justification for political rule rests on a subject possessing a mandate to rule from Heaven.

thesis for this Element is that the central metaphysics of some Eastern traditions surveyed can be rendered in a logically consistent way with the central metaphysics of Classical Theism. Hopefully tentatively, our reader can agree with us that we've done that much so far.

Nonetheless, we would like to go back to Ivanhoe's interpretation that *Tian* is not God but something impersonal that nonetheless engages with the world in an active way. We wonder if Ivanhoe's hesitancy with connecting *Tian* with theism relates to a very anthropomorphic conception of God where God is fundamentally a person as you and I are persons. *Tian* isn't a person, at least, not in a univocal sense of the term. If this is all Ivanhoe means by *Tian* not being related to God, we Classical Theists can agree with him that *Tian* shouldn't be read theistically. Rather, *Tian* is the grounding of goodness, the explanation of why humans are good, and the overall guiding force in nature. But this is consistent with what Classical Theists believe about God. God isn't fundamentally a person as we are persons. Rather He is the explanation for why there is something rather than nothing and He is identical to goodness itself. So, while one might argue that Confucianism is consistent with both Classical Theism and Neo-Classical Theism, it might be that the Classical Theistic view is in a better position than the Neo-Classical Theistic view in making sense of the immanent and more impersonal intuitions about *Tian* that are reflected in the contemporary literature. Perhaps one wants to argue that *Tian* is discussed anthropomorphically in the Confucian canon so that *Tian* can't be read consistently with the Classical Theist view. The Classical Theist has a response. In the same way Christians give an analogical reading to their Scripture, a Classical Theist Confucian can give a similar treatment to the Confucian canon. If the Christian Scriptures state that God possesses knowledge, the Classical Theist doesn't think we are committed to believing that God has what we mean by knowledge. She understands knowledge analogically. Similarly, the Confucian can make the same move. If a text reads that *Tian* has knowledge or judges, we can understand that this is an analogy. There is a consistent reading to be had. Saying this, it seems that most interpreters have more impersonal intuitions about *Tian*. So this issue is unlikely to be raised. Having now discussed Confucianism and Classical Theism, we turn to our last engagement.

5 Daoism and Classical Theism

5.1 The Dao

What is the Dao (道)? Is the Dao something positive or negative? Is it in nature or beyond nature? Is the Dao God? Herein, we give what we take to be two important chapters of *Daodejing* as it relates to defining the Dao:

Chapter 14

Look, it cannot be seen – it is beyond form.
Listen, it cannot be heard – it is beyond sound.
Grasp, it cannot be held – it is intangible.
These three are indefinable;
Therefore they are joined in one.

From above it is not bright;
From below it is not dark:
An unbroken thread beyond description.
It returns to nothingness.
The form of the formless,
The image of the imageless,
It is called indefinable and beyond imagination.

Stand before it and there is no beginning.
Follow it and there is no end.
Stay with the ancient Tao,
Move with the present.
Knowing the ancient beginning is the essence of Tao.
  (Lao, 1991)

Wang Bi interprets this passage as saying that the Dao is what entities are based on. He interprets the Dao not having form to mean that the Dao is 'no-thing:

> One wishes to say that it does not exist? [The fact still remains] that entities are based on it for their completion. One wants to say it exists? [The fact remains] that it does not show form. That is why [the text] says: "shape of shapeless, appearance of the no-thing.' (Wang Bi, 2003, p. 163)

Summarizing the last portion of the chapter, Wang Bi states the following:

> The featureless and nameless is the ancestor of the ten thousand kinds of entities. Although the present and antiquity are not the same, although times have changed and customs have changed, there definitely is no one who has not based himself on this [featureless and nameless] by way of completing their regulated order. (Wang Bi, 2003, p. 164)

Once again, the Dao is seen as the featureless ancestor of all entities. The Dao is the source of order and design. Yet, the Dao lacks form or name.

Chapter 25

Something mysteriously formed,
Born before heaven and earth.
In the silence and the void,
Standing alone and unchanging,
Ever present and in motion.
Perhaps it is the mother of ten thousand things.

> I do not know its name.
> Call it Tao.
> For lack of a better word, I call it great.
>
> Being great, it flows.
> It flows far away.
> Having gone far, it returns.
>
> Therefore, "Tao is great;
> Heaven is great;
> Earth is great;
> The king is also great."
> These are the four great powers of the universe,
> And the king is one of them.
>
> Man follows the earth.
> Earth follows heaven.
> Heaven follows the Tao.
> Tao follows what is natural. (Lao Tsu and Wang Bi, 2003, p. 164)

Wang Bi interprets the Dao flowing far away and returning, as the Dao having an eternal nature which it returns to (Wang Bi, 2003, p. 202). The Dao mysteriously forms and is born before all ages. Yet, it is ever present and in motion. According to Ronnie Littlejohn, Wang Bi thinks that 'The Non-Being has neither form, nor shadow; it conforms completely to what surrounds it . . . Its form is invisible: it is the Supreme Being" (Little John, *IEP*). In Hans-Georg Moeller's *Daoism Explained*, Moeller defines the Dao as a 'perfect pattern of order that is constituted by *wu* and you, by nonpresence and presence' (Moeller, 2001, p. 137). Due to the Dao being the eternal and invisible supreme being, pattern and grounding of all things, and yet, it is beyond things, our attentive reader might again be tempted to see commonality between God and the Dao. Perhaps the Dao really is God or the Buddha nature, or Brahman after all.

5.2 Reductionism

Moeller would not be happy with the above comparison. While the God of Classical Theism and the Dao are ineffable, according to Moller, they are ineffable for different reasons. This has to do with how he interprets ineffability in the Christian tradition. For Moeller, God is ineffable because there is nothing in the world that can accurately represent Him, 'whereas the Dao is ineffable because it is nonpresent' (Moeller, 2001, p. 148).

Utilizing the work of third-century philosopher He Yan, Moeller compares the Dao to the hub of a wheel (Moeller, 2001, p. 145). The hub of the wheel is essential for the wheel to function; it connects the spokes to the wheel's circumference. Yet, the hub is a nonpresence of sorts. As Moeller puts it, 'In the Daoist semiotics of presence, names and the nameless, presence and nonpresence, coexist.' Yet, according to Moeller, 'The Dao cannot be given a name because it has no qualities.' It doesn't belong to the realm of interplay between names and forms (Moeller, 2001, p. 145). So, the Dao is nonpresence, lacks qualities, and doesn't belong to the interplay of our world. This is a far cry from a personal God who engages with creation, right? So, case closed; the Dao cannot be read interchangeably with God.

Not so fast. At the start of the common era, some interpreters of Daoism developed a religion of the Dao. For a religious Daoist, Daoism isn't simply nonexistence, the Dao is identified as the highest deity. Once again, our reader might be unimpressed. You have religious Daoism and true Daoist philosophy. What we need to do is show that the metaphysics of Daoism the philosophy is consistent with the metaphysics of Classical Theism, not the metaphysics of the later religion. These are two separate things, right?

5.3 Digging Up the Dao

Scholarship on Daoism made a turn in 1993. In China's Hubei Province, bamboo-slip manuscripts dating back to approximately 300 BC were discovered, including *The Taiyi Sheng Shui/Da Yi Sheng Shui*, or 'The Great One Gives Birth to the Waters.' This text informs us how ancient Daoist cosmologies relate to theistic belief. Translated by Sarah Allan, slips 1–8 read:

> The Great One produced water (*Da Yi sheng shui* 大一生水). The water, on return, assisted (*fu*) the Great One, thus forming (*cheng* 成) the sky (*Tian* 天). The sky, returning, assisted the Great One, thus forming the earth (*di* 地). The sky and earth again assisted one another (1), thus forming the numinous and the luminous (*shen ming* 神明). The numinous and the luminous again assisted one another, thus forming *yin* and *yang* (陰陽). *Yin* and *yang* again assisted one another, thus forming the four seasons (*si shi* 四). The four seasons (2) again assisted one another, thus forming cold and heat (*cang ran* 倉然). Cold and heat again assisted one another, thus forming moisture and aridity (*shi zao* 濕燥). Moisture and aridity again assisted one another, formed a year (3) and that was all. Therefore, a year is that which moisture and aridity produced. Moisture and aridity are that which cold and heat produced. Cold and heat are that which the four seasons produced. The four seasons (4) are that which *yin* and *yang* produced. *Yin* and *yang* are that which the numinous and the luminous produced. The numinous and the luminous are that which the sky and earth produced. Sky and earth (5) are that which the Great One produced. For this reason, the Great One hides in (*cang* 藏) water and moves with the seasons. Circling and [beginning again, it takes itself as] (6) the mother of the myriad living

things. Waning and waxing, it takes itself as the guideline of the myriad living things. It is what the sky cannot exterminate, what the earth (7) cannot bury, that which yin and yang cannot form. The gentleman who knows this is called [a sage]. (Allan, 2003, p. 261)

Allan argues that what this shows is that Daoism as a philosophy and Daoism as a religion, are not so separate after all (Allan, 2003, p. 285).

Allan argues that 'The Great One' is a personal creator:

"The Great One produced water." The first character, transcribed as *tai* 太 in the *Guodian Chu mu zhujian*, is actually written as *da* 大 on the bamboo slips, as noted above. *Tai (Da)* means "ancestral" as well as "great," and the epithet designates the first ancestor of a lineage, as in *taizu* 太祖, or *taiwang* 太王—the founding king's father. Thus, Tai (Da) Yi is the "Ancestral" or "Grand" One—the ultimate ancestor who was the progenitor of the sky and earth. (Allan, 2003, p. 262)

The Great One was identified not only with the Dao but also with the Pole Star (Allan, 2003, pp. 251–252). It seems likely, historically at least, that some philosophical Daoists have been theists. It would be weird if there was a history of philosophical Daoists who interpreted the Dao to functionally be God, and yet, all stripes of theism are actually inconsistent with Daosim. It at least wasn't plausibly inconsistent with religious Daoists' interpretation of Daoism and likely their reading of the *Daodejing*. It appears then that there is a basis for interpreting the Dao in a transcendent way.

5.4 Moeller Revisited

But what are we to make of the Dao being non-presence, lacking qualities, and not being in the realm of interplay? Given what we've said so far in this Element, we don't think what Moeller says is inconsistent with Classical Theism. Once again, we can agree with both Shankara and Moeller that ultimate reality is qualityless. While it is true that the Dao is presented as non-presence, it also is presented as the source and order of things. It is even perceived as a no-entity or no-thing which is responsible for existence in some way.

The analogy of the Dao being like the hub of wheel is an interesting analogy. It would be wrong to say that there is no hub or that the hub doesn't exist in any sense. Sure, it doesn't exist in the same way the spokes of the wheel exist. But it is what makes the existence of spokes possible. In the same way, again, God is no-thing, and yet, He is what makes things possible. God doesn't exist in the same way that things exist. God isn't a causal agent as you and I are causal agents. God isn't part of the interplay of our reality. He is rather the reason why any interplay exists. As discussed in Section 1, when Classical Theists say that God causes X, it is more precise to say that God causes* X. God doesn't cause and act in the way things interact. Given this, far from being opposed to Classical Theism, we think the metaphysics espoused in Daoism can be read in a way that is logically consistent with the metaphysics of Classical Theism. In fact, Davide Andrea Zappulli has even recently argued that Daoism has a creation story too (Zappulli, forthcoming).

5.5 Conclusion

We are now in a position to summarize what has been argued for. We spent the first chapter clarifying what the metaphysics of Classical Theism are. We paid special attention to the doctrines of simplicity, immutability, impassibility, and divine ineffability. We made clear that the sort of theism we are interested in, Classical Theism, doesn't view God as a thing but that which is beyond the realm of existent things; God is beyond being. Doing so, we distinguished Classical Theism from a position called Neo-Classical Theism. After briefly surveying relevant objections to Classical Theism, we argued that our project is tenable. This allowed us to argue that the central metaphysics endorsed by various Eastern philosophical traditions can be interpreted in a consistent way with the central metaphysical theses of Classical Theism.

In the second section, we first looked at the Buddhist tradition. We clarified that the central metaphysical theses of Buddhism are the impermanence thesis, the interdependence thesis, and the emptiness thesis. After clarifying that these theses applied to things, we argued that given Classical Theism, God is not a thing, and the Buddhist theses don't apply to God. If, of course, one was convinced that the central theses *did* apply to that which is beyond the existent realm, we argued that the Buddhist, utilizing a skillful means hermeneutic, can argue that the theses were only temporally endorsed in a radically unrestricted sense, in order to help others achieve enlightenment without taking such language to be indicative of how things really are. We followed this discussion up by arguing that the Shentong tradition makes claims similar as to the ones we made.

In the third section we argued that there is no such things as a singular, monolithic religious tradition that goes by the name Hinduism. Rather, there are various Hindu worldviews. While some Hindu views are straightforwardly theistic, we set out to argue that the central metaphysics of Shankara's

Advaita Vedānta tradition could be read in a consistent way with the central metaphysics of Classical Theism. We argued that while in this tradition God is understood to be qualityless and impersonal, given the doctrine of simplicity and the doctrine of analogy, a Classical Theist could also endorse that God is qualityless and in some analogical sense, impersonal. Given that God is not a thing among other things, it would also be wrong to count God as a separate item or object and take the universe to be another object. There simply aren't two kinds or types of things, God and the universe. Finally, we argued that while the statement 'God is the material cause of the universe' is rather mysterious in the Advaita tradition, the Classical Theist might nevertheless be able to endorse this view, at least analogically.

Next up, in Section 4, we moved further East. We argued that the concept of *Tian* found both within Confucius and Mencius can be read interchangeably with God. *Tian* is the source of reality and the cause of virtue. *Tian* can also punish and guide humanity. There is a plausible case to make that *Tian* isn't purely the physical world but that which transcends it. We then argued that interpretations which see *Tian* neither as God nor as the natural world, but as some mysterious force, can be made sense of on Classical Theist grounds. *Tian* isn't an anthropomorphic deity, but the metaphysical grounding of all things.

Finally, in our last section, we looked at key passages in the *Daodejing* where the Dao is conveyed as impassible, ineffable, eternal, and the source of order. We argued looking at the Dao this way was also consistent with how Classical Theists conceive of God. Objecting to this claim, we engaged Moeller's argument that while the Dao and God are both ineffable, they are ineffable for very different reasons. Specifically, Moeller interprets the Dao to be non-presence, akin to a hub on a wheel, and thus qualityless. We argued that Moeller's rejection of the Dao being compared to God likely relates to an interpretation that God is an object that is to be represented. We argued that there were readings of non-presence which are consistent with the metaphysics of Classical Theism.

Having said all this, we hope to have convinced our reader that the central metaphysics of various Eastern philosophical traditions *can* be rendered in a logically consistent way with the central metaphysics of Classical Theism. What we didn't discuss, however, is that it seems rather odd if metaphysical systems found throughout different time periods and in different places of the world can be synthesized into a global picture of reality. It might be the case that the central metaphysical theses discussed in this Element are all explicitly endorsed by the respective traditions. If Buddhism, Advaita Vedānta, Daosim, and Confucianism share the same metaphysics of the Absolute, one might think this calls for an explanation. As Perry Schmidt-Leukel argues, the great religious traditions are fractal patterns (Schmidt-Leukel, 2024). A thorough explication and defense of this claim warrants its own volume and should be taken up by scholars. But such an explanation will have to wait for another day.

References

Abe, Masao. "Non-Being and Mu: The Metaphysical Nature of Negativity in the East and the West." In *Zen and Western Thought*, edited by William R. LaFleur, 127. Honolulu: University of Hawai'i Press, 1985.

——. "Sunyata as Formless Form: Plato and Mahayana Buddhism." In *Zen and Comparative Studies*, edited by Steven Heine, 139. Honolulu: University of Hawai'i Press, 1997.

Allan, Sarah. "The Great One, Water, and the *Laozi*: New Light from Guodian." *T'oung Pao*, Second Series 89, no. 4/5 (2003): 261.

Ames, Roger. *Confucian Role of Ethics: A Vocabulary*. Hong Kong: Hong Kong University Press, 2011.

Ames, Roger, and Henry Rosemont. *The Analects of Confucius: A Philosophical Translation*. New York: Random House, 1999.

Anderson, James. *Paradox in Christian Theology: An Analysis of Its Presence, Character, and Epistemic Status*. Milton Keynes: Paternoster, 2007.

Anselm. *Monologion; and, Proslogion: With the Replies of Gaunilo and Anselm*. Translated by Thomas Williams. Indianapolis: Hackett, 1996.

Aquinas, Thomas. *Summa Theologica: Complete English Edition in Five Volumes*. Westminster: Christian Classics, 1981.

Aristotle. *Metaphysics*. With introduction and notes by C. D. C. Reeve. Indianapolis: Hackett, 2016.

Baldwin, Erik. *Fully Informed Reasonable Disagreement and Tradition Based Perspectivalism*. Bristol, CT: Peeters-Leuven, 2016.

Baldwin, Erik, and Tyler Dalton McNabb. *Plantingian Religious Epistemology and World Religions: Problems and Prospects*. Lanham: Lexington Press, 2018.

Barrett, Justin. *Science, Religion, and Theology: From Human Minds to Divine Minds*. Philadelphia: Templeton Press, 2011.

Bergmann, Michael. "Skeptical Theism and the Problem of Evil." In *The Oxford Handbook of Philosophical Theology*, edited by Thomas Flint and Michael Rea, 377–378. Oxford: Oxford University Press, 2011.

Brown, Joshua. *Aquinas and Early Chinese Masters: Chinese Philosophy and Catholic Theology*. Washington, DC: Catholic University of America Press, 2024.

Burns, Elizabeth. *Continental Philosophy of Religion*. Cambridge: Cambridge University Press, 2019.

Burton, David. *Buddhism: A Contemporary Philosophical Investigation*. Basingstoke: Taylor & Francis, 2017.

Casti, Filippo and Simon Hewitt. "Grammatical Thomism: An Introduction." *International Journal of Philosophy and Theology* 85 (2024): 1–7.

Clark, Kelly James, and Justin Winslett. *A Spiritual Geography of Early Chinese Thought: Gods, Ancestors, and Afterlife.* London: Bloomsbury, 2023.

Cline, Eric. *The Analects: A Guide.* Oxford: Oxford University Press, 2021.

Craig, William Lane. *Time and Eternity: Exploring God's Relationship to Time.* Wheaton, IL: Crossway Books, 2001.

Creel, Herrlee Clessner. "Was Confucius and Agnostic?" *T'oung Pao* 29 (1932): 55–99.

Crow, Sheryl. *Everyday Is a Winding Road: Sheryl Crow.* Hollywood: A&M Records, 1996, track 9.

Davies, Brian. *The Reality of God and the Problem of Evil.* London: Continuum Press, 2006.

"Letters from America." *New Blackfriars* 84 (2003): 371–384.

D'Ettore, Domenic. *Analogy After Aquinas: Logical Problems, Thomistic Answers.* Washington, DC: Catholic University of America Press, 2019, 33–60.

DeVito, Michael, and Tyler Dalton McNabb. "Divine Foreknowledge and Human Freedom: Embracing the Paradox." *International Journal for Philosophy of Religion* 90 (2021): 93–107.

Dölpopa, Gyaltsen. *The Buddha from Dolpo: A Study on the Life and Thought of the Tibetan Master Dölpopa Sherab Gyaltsen.* Translated by Cyrus Stearns. Ithaca: Snow Lion Press, 2010.

Duby, Steven J. *Divine Simplicity: A Dogmatic Account.* New York: T&T Clark, 2016.

Slingerland, Edward. *The Essential Analects: Selected Passages with Traditional Commentary.* Indianapolis: Hackett, 2006.

Eno, Robert. *The Confucian Creation of Heaven: Philosophy and Defense of Ritual Mastery.* New York: SUNY Press, 1990.

Feser, Edward. *Scholastic Metaphysics: A Contemporary Introduction.* Neunkirchen-Seelscheid: Editiones Scholasticiae, 2014.

Feser, Edward. "The Neo-Classical Challenge to Classical Theism." *Philosophy Compass* 17, no. 8 (2022): 1–9.

Frazier, Jessica. *Hindu Worldviews: Theories of Self, Ritual, and Reality.* London: Bloomsbury, 2017.

Garfield, Jay L. *Engaging Buddhism: Why It Matters to Philosophy.* Oxford: Oxford University Press, 2014.

Gilson, Etienne. *The Christian Philosophy of St. Thomas Aquinas.* Notre Dame: University of Notre Dame Press, 1956.

Granet, Marcel. *La Pensée Chinoise*. Paris: Albin Michel, 1934.

Hall, David, and Roger Ames. *Thinking through Confucius*. New York: SUNY Press, 1987.

Harrison, Victoria. *Eastern Philosophy*. Cambridge: Cambridge University Press, 2022.

Eastern Philosophy: The Basics. New York: Routledge, 2013.

Hart, David Bentley. *The Experience of God: Being, Consciousness, Bliss*. New Haven: Yale University Press, 2014.

Herbert, Frank. *Dune*. Philadelphia: Chilton Books, 1965.

Hewitt, Simon 2020. *Negative Theology and Philosophical Analysis: Only the Splendour of Life* London: Palgrave MacMillan.

Hirota, Dennis, trans. *The Collected Works of Shinran*, Vol. II. Kyoto: Jodo Shinshu Hongwanji, 1997.

Hornbeck, Ryan, Barrett, Justin, and Kang, Madeleine. *Religious Cognition in China: "Homo Religiosus" and the Dragon*. Switzlerand: Springer, 2017.

Hua, Hsüan. *The Sixth Patriarch's Dharma Jewel Platform Sutra: Liuzu Da Shi Fa Bao Tan Jing*, ed. Martin Verhoeven. Ukiah, CA: Buddhist Text Translation Society, 2014.

Ivanhoe, Philip. "Heaven as a Source for Ethical Warrant in Early Confucianism." *Dao* 6, (2007): 211–220.

Lamont, John. "Aquinas on Divine Simplicity." *The Monist* 80, no. 4 (1997): 521–538.

Lao, Tzu. *Tao Te Ching*. Translated by Gia-Fu Feng and Jane English. London: Wildwood House, 1991.

Leibniz, Gottfried Wilhelm *Die philosophischen Schriften*. 7 vols. Edited by C. I. Gerhardt. Hildesheim: Georg Olms, 1965.

Leibniz, Gottfried Wilhelm. *Philosophical Essays*. Translated by Roger Ariew and Daniel Garber. Indianapolis: Hackett, 1989.

Legge, James. *The Religions of China*. New York: Charles Scribner's Sons, 1881.

Mathes, Klaus-Dieter. "Taranatha's 'Twenty-One Differences with Regard to the Profound Meaning': Comparing the Views of the Two Gzan Ston Masters Dol Po Pa and Sakya MChog." *Journal of the International Association of Buddhist Studies* 27 (2004): 285–328.

McNabb, Tyler Dalton, and Erik Baldwin. *Classical Theism and Buddhism: Connecting Metaphysical and Ethical Systems*. London: Bloomsbury, 2022.

McNabb, Tyler Dalton. "The Shentong Tradition and Classical Theism: A Synthesis?" *Philosophy East and West* (forthcoming).

McNabb, Tyler Dalton. "The Problem of Evil for Buddhists: Developing Transcendental Responses." *Agatheos: European Journal for Philosophy of Religion* 1, no. 2 (2024): 46–53.

McNabb, Tyler Dalton and Erik Baldwin. "The Stigmata, Rainbow Bodies, and Hume's Argument against Miracles." *Journal of Philosophy and Religion Society of Thailand* 19, no. 1 (2024): 83–93.

Mencius. *Mencius*, trl. Irene Bloom. New York: Colombia University Press, 2009.

Michelson, Jared. "Thomistic Divine Simplicity and Its Analytic Detractors: Can One Affirm Divine Aseity and Goodness without Simplicity?" *The Heythrop Journal* 63, no. 6, (2022): 1140–1162.

Moeller, Hans-Georg. *Daoism Explained: From the Dream of the Butterfly to the Fishnet Allegory*. Chicago: Open Court Press, 2001.

Mullins, Ryan T. *The End of the Timeless God*. Oxford: Oxford University Press, 2016. https://doi.org/10.1093/acprof:oso/9780198755180.001.0001.

Murphy, Mark C. *God's Own Ethics: Norms of Divine Agency and the Argument from Evil*. New York: Oxford University Press, 2017.

Ñāṇamoli, Bhikku and Bodhi Bhikku. *The Middle Length Discourses of the Buddha: A New Translation of the Majjhima NikāYa*. Boston: Wisdom Publications in association with the Barre Center for Buddhist Studies, 1995.

Patil, Parimal. *Against a Hindu God: A Buddhist Philosophy of Religion in India*. New York: Columbia University Press, 2009.

Peckham, John C. *Divine Attributes: Knowing the Covenantal God of Scripture*. Grand Rapids: Baker Academic, 2021.

"Classical Theism and Theological Method: A Critical Inquiry." *Religions* 15, no. 8 (2024): 915. https://doi.org/10.3390/rel15080915.

Plantinga, Alvin. *Does God Have a Nature?* Milwaukee: Marquette University Press, 1980.

Plantinga, Alvin. *The Nature of Necessity*. Oxford: Clarendon Press, 1992.

Plantinga, Alvin. *Does God Have a Nature*. Milwaukee: Marquette University Press, 2007, 47.

Plato. *The Republic*, 509b. In *Plato: Complete Works*, edited by John M. Cooper, 971–1223. Indianapolis: Hackett, 1997.

Prabhavananda, Swami, and Christopher Isherwood. *Shankara's Crest Jewel of Discrimination*. Hollywood: Vedanta Press, 1975.

Panchuk, Michelle. "The Simplicity of Divine Ideas: Theistic Conceptual Realism and the Doctrine of Divine Simplicity." *Religious Studies* 57, no. 3 (2021): 385–402. https://doi.org/10.1017/S0034412519000301.

Robson, Gregory J. "Reconsidering the Necessary Beings of Aquinas's Third Way." *European Journal for Philosophy of Religion* 4, no. 1 (2012): 219–241.

Rambachan, Anatanand. *A Hindu Theology of Liberation: Not-Two Is Not-One*. New York: SUNY Press, 2015.

Rooney, James. "Unknowing: Christian and Buddhist Soteriological Epistemology." *British Journal for the History of Philosophy* (forthcoming).

Rowe, William L. "The Problem of Evil and Some Varieties of Atheism." *American Philosophical Quarterly* 16, no. 4 (1979): 335–341.

Shankara, Adi. *Shankara's Crest Jewel of Discrimination*. Hollywood: Vedanta Press, 1975.

Shankaracharya, Adi. *Aparokshanubhuti: Or Self-Realization of Sri Sankaracharya*. Translated by Swami Vimuktananda. Hollywood: Vedanta Press, 1938.

Schwartz, Benjamin. *The World Thought in Ancient China*. Cambrdge: Belknap Press, 1985.

Schmid, Joseph C., and Mullins, Ryan T. "The Aloneness Argument against Classical Theism." *Religious Studies* 58, no. 2, (2022): 401–419. https://doi.org/10.1017/S0034412520000554.

Scotus, Duns. *Vol. III: Ordinatio I*, Distinctio 3 (Città del Vaticano, 1954).

Schmidt-Leukel, Perry. *The Celestial Web: Buddhism and Christianity: A Different Comparison*. Translated by David West. Maryknoll, NY: Orbis Books, 2024.

Sheehy, Michael, and Klaus-Dieter Mathes, eds. *The Other Emptiness: Rethinking the Zhentong Buddhist Discourse in Tibet*. Albany: SUNY Press, 2019.

Shinran. *The Collected Works of Shinran*, Vol. I. Translated by Dennis Hirota. Kyoto: Jodo Shinshu Hongwanji, 1997.

Shree Swami, and Yeats William Butler . trans. "Chhandogya-Upanishad." In *The Ten Principal Upanishads*. New Delhi: Rupa Publications, 2003.

Sijuwade, Joshua Reginald. "The Metaphysics of Theism: A Classical and Neo-Classical Synthesis. *Religions*." 12, no. 11 (2021): 967. https://doi.org/10.3390/rel12110967.

Soars, Daniel. *The World and God Are Not-Two: A Hindu and Christian Conversation*. New York: Fordham Press, 2023.

Stoker, Valarie. "Madhva (1238–1317)." *Internet Encyclopedia of Philosophy*. Accessed January 6, 2025. https://iep.utm.edu/madhva/.

Swinburne, Richard. *The Coherence of Theism*. Oxford: Clarendon Press, 1977.

Thanissaro, Bhikku. *The Mind Like Fire Unbound*. Barrie: Dhamma Dana Publications, 2016.

Tilakaratne, Asanga. "The Ultimate Buddhist Religious Goal, Nirvana, and its Implications for Buddhist-Christian Dual Belonging." In *Buddhist-Christian Dual Belonging: Affirmations, Objections, and Explorations*, edited by Gavin D'Costa and Ross Thompson, 100–101. Farnham: Ashgate, 2016.

Tennent, Timothy. *Christianity at the Religious Roundtable: Evangelical in Conversation with Hinduism, Buddhism, and Islam*. Grand Rapids: Baker Academic, 2002.

Tomaszewski, Christopher. "Collapsing the Modal Collapse Argument: On an Invalid Argument against Divine Simplicity." *Analysis* 79, no. 2 (2019): 275–284.

Trl. Bhikkhu Ñāṇamoli and Bhikkhu, Bodhi. *The Middle Length Discourses of the Buddha*. Somerville: Wisdom Publications, 2015.

Wahlberg, Åke. "God's Necessary Existence: A Thomistic perspective." *International Journal for Philosophy of Religion* 95, no. 2 (2024): 131–152.

Wang Bi. "Commentary." In *A Chinese Reading of the Daodejing: Wang Bi's Commentary on the Laozi with Critical Text and Translation*, edited by Rudolf Wagner, 107–118. Albany: SUNY Press, 2003.

Ward, Keith. *Religion and Revelation*. Oxford: Clarendon Press, 1994.

Westerhoff, Jan. *Nāgārjuna's Madhyamaka: A Philosophical Introduction*. Oxford: Oxford University Press, 2010.

Westerhoff, Jan. *The Golden Age of Indian Buddhist Philosophy*. 1st ed. Oxford: Oxford University Press, 2018.

Williams, Paul. *An Unexpected Way: On Converting from Buddhism to Catholicism*. London: T&T Clark, 2002.

Yang, Fenggang. "Confucianism as Civil Religion." In *Confucianism, A Habit of the Heart: Bellah, Civil Religion, and East Asia*, edited by Philip J. Ivanhoe and Sungmoon Kim, 30. New York: SUNY Press, 2016.

Yagi, Seiichi, and Leonard Swidler. *A Bridge to Buddhist-Christian Dialogue*. Mahwah, NJ: Paulist Press, 1990.

Yu, Chun-Fang. "Eye on Religion: Miracles in the Chinese Buddhist Tradition." *Southern Medical Journal* 100 (2007): 1243–1250.

Zappulli, Davide. "The Metaphysics of Creation in the Daodejing." *Ergo* (forthcoming).

Acknowledgements

As for now, I (Tyler) would like to thank my family for giving me time and inspiration to write this volume. Thank you, Priscilla, Eden, Elijah, Ezra, Eva-Maria, Ezekiel, Evangeline, and Exavier. Yes, all of the "E" names are my children. I'd also like to thank Pope Francis (may he send us powerful prayers from heaven) and Pope Leo XIV for emphasizing the importance of interreligious dialogue. Finally, I'd like to thank the developers of *Wukong* for making me wish I was back in China, especially as I bounced back and forth from playing it and writing this volume.

(Erik) This volume builds on and extends many ideas and themes that Tyler and I have been working on for years. I'm grateful to have built up a considerable amount of co-authored material with you, Tyler. May our research and especially our friendship continue to be fruitful. I'd like to thank God for the gift of my wife, Melanie, and my daughter, Naomi. Melanie, may you be blessed with health, happiness, and peace. Naomi, may the Lord make His face shine upon you, and be gracious to you; may the Lord lift up His countenance upon you and give you peace. I dedicate this Element to my mom, Anita. Lord, thank you for the gift of my mother. Bless her with health, joy, and peace. May she always be surrounded by your love and grace. Amen.

Cambridge Elements =

Global Philosophy of Religion

Yujin Nagasawa
University of Oklahoma

Yujin Nagasawa is Kingfisher College Chair of the Philosophy of Religion and Ethics and Professor of Philosophy at the University of Oklahoma. He is the author of *The Problem of Evil for Atheists* (2024), *Maximal God: A New Defence of Perfect Being Theism* (2018), *Miracles: A Very Short Introduction* (2018), *The Existence of God: A Philosophical Introduction* (2011), and *God and Phenomenal Consciousness* (2008), along with numerous articles. He is the editor-in-chief of *Religious Studies* and served as the president of the British Society for the Philosophy of Religion from 2017 to 2019.

About the Series

This Cambridge Elements series provides concise and structured overviews of a wide range of religious beliefs and practices, with an emphasis on global, multi-faith viewpoints. Leading scholars from diverse cultural backgrounds and geographical regions explore topics and issues that have been overlooked by Western philosophy of religion.

Cambridge Elements =

Global Philosophy of Religion

Elements in the Series

Afro-Brazilian Religions
José Eduardo Porcher

The African Mood Perspective on God and the Problem of Evil
Ada Agada

Contemporary Pagan Philosophy
Eric Steinhart

Semi-Secular Worldviews and the Belief in Something Beyond
Carl-Johan Palmqvist and Francis Jonbäck

Zoroastrianism and Contemporary Philosophy
Daniel Nolan

Karma and Rebirth in Hinduism
Swami Medhananda

Religious Naturalism
John Bishop and Ken Perszyk

The Notion of Vitality in African Philosophy of Religion
Aribiah David Attoe and Amara Esther Chimakonam

Eastern Philosophy and Classical Theism
Tyler Dalton McNabb and Erik Baldwin

A full series listing is available at: www.cambridge.org/EGPR

For EU product safety concerns, contact us at Calle de José Abascal, 56–1°,
28003 Madrid, Spain or eugpsr@cambridge.org.

www.ingramcontent.com/pod-product-compliance
Lightning Source LLC
LaVergne TN
LVHW020006080526
838200LV00081B/4410